AF469344

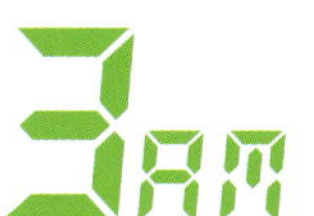
3AM

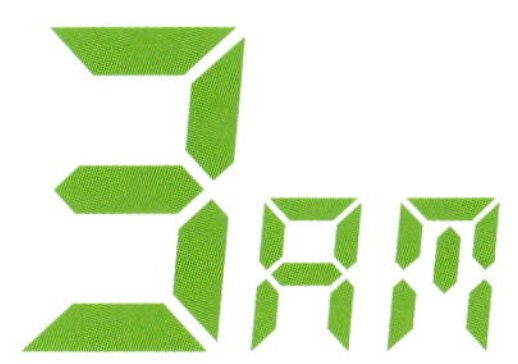


# wonder, paranoia and the restless night

Published on the occasion of the exhibition *3am: wonder, paranoia and the restless night,* curated for the Bluecoat by Angela Kingston, with additional research by Bryan Biggs and Sara-Jayne Parsons.

Exhibition dates:

28 September – 24 November 2013
The Bluecoat, School Lane, Liverpool L1 3BX
13 December 2013 – 2 March 2014
Chapter, Market Road, Cardiff CF5 1QE
April – June 2014
Newlyn Art Gallery & The Exchange, Princes Street, Penzance, Cornwall TR18 2NL
20 September – December 2014
Ferens Art Gallery, Queen Victoria Square, Kingston Upon Hull HU1 3RA

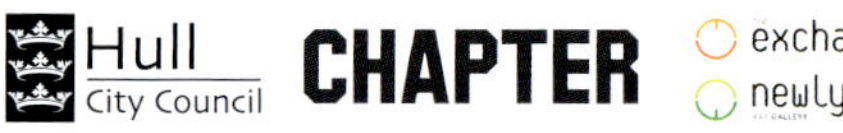


Published 2013 by

Liverpool University Press,
4 Cambridge Street,
Liverpool,
L69 7ZU

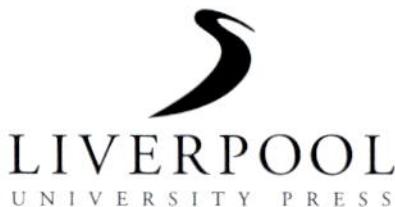


and

The Bluecoat,
School Lane,
Liverpool,
L1 3BX

**the Bluecoat.**

ISBN 978-1-84631-957-0



Cover image: Dornith Doherty, *Dry Creek* (detail), 2012. Archival pigment photograph, 76.2 × 101.6 cm. Courtesy the artist, Holly Johnson Gallery, and McMurtrey Gallery.

Designed by Carnegie Book Production

# CONTENTS

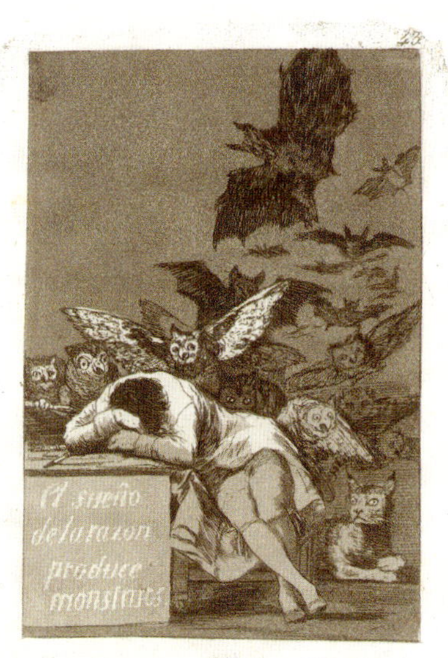


Francisco de Goya (1746–1828), *The Sleep of Reason Produces Monsters (El sueño de la razón produce monstrous)*, 1799
Etching, aquatint, drypoint and burin, 21.5 × 15 cm
New York, Metropolitan Museum of Art. Gift of M. Knoedler & Co., 1918. Acc.n.: 18.64(43) © 2013. Image copyright The Metropolitan Museum of Art/Art Resource/Scala, Florence. *©Photo SCALA, Florence*

# FOREWORD

## Bryan Biggs

Whilst writing this foreword, I Google *current thinking about the night*, which throws up random observations, like 'night owls score higher than morning people on general intelligence'. It's the early hours, but bathed in the computer screen's constant glow this could be any time, the digital clock in the corner unobtrusive and silent. Nowadays the traditional time for winding down is as likely to wind us up: work-related emails pinging in past midnight, lost in labyrinthine Internet searches, wasted hours of YouTube diversions, regretting another impulsive late night Amazon purchase. As the economic treadmill of our globalised world turns endlessly – even through the night – the idea of the nocturnal hours providing 'temporary social distance'[1], a place of refuge from the incessancy of contemporary life, seems threatened by this technological invasion, encouraged as it is by our love affair with instant communication (and recent research suggests that it's the waking hours too that are similarly affected by our digital obsession[2]). Might this encroachment however also lead us to regard the still of the night as an increasingly precious commodity, and to place even greater value on the night as a time of possibility?

As the shadow side of our daylight existence, with its regulated time, the night in contrast is unconstrained; and the wee, small hours in particular can offer a sense of freedom – but they can also be full of dread. The insomniac, for instance, wonders if day will ever come, there is a sense of reaching the nadir, of being in a dark place. It's a time when the mind races, a demonic time of ghouls and nocturnal creatures, of nightmares, loneliness and death. It can also be a time for euphoric release, for dreams and adventure, for creativity and imagination, for lawlessness and transgression. A metaphorical reflection perhaps of the uncertain times in which we live, might three o'clock in the morning – the hour most acutely associated with nocturnal otherness – be considered the current *zeitgeist?*

It was with these thoughts that freelance curator Angela Kingston approached the Bluecoat when she outlined her concept for an exhibition that would explore the far night. 3 a.m. seemed to be fertile territory for the artist, and through a process of dialogue around Angela's rich thematic and a core list of potential artists, an imaginative and compelling exhibition, *3am: wonder, paranoia and the restless night*, has taken shape. We all wanted it to capture something of the strangeness of this hour and the extraordinary range of states and experiences – psychological, sociological, natural and astronomical – that it witnesses. These are reflected in the work of twenty two contemporary UK and international artists who step into the night to create paintings, drawings, videos, photographs, sound works and sculptures, some of them made especially for the exhibition.

In tandem with developing the exhibition, Angela gathered writings about the night – extracted from scientific, sociological, philosophical, poetic and fictional sources – and a selection of these is brought together here, alongside new essays commissioned for the publication, which is intended as a sort of reader to accompany the exhibition, as well as functioning in its own right. Of the three new texts, Angela's introduces her thinking behind the project as she discusses, with the same passion that informed her conception of the exhibition, the work of the artists selected. Fiction writer Ailsa Cox's vivid short story, written specially for this publication, interweaves three narratives all taking place at 3 a.m. Photography is prominent in the exhibition, and the Bluecoat's Exhibition Curator Sara-Jayne Parson's perceptive essay provides a historical context for work in this medium, which literally uses light to conjure images from the dark.

Broadening the book's scope further, I have drawn up a playlist of popular, and some not so popular songs relating to 3 a.m., an attempt at an insomniac's top twenty. Alongside a small number of well-known art historical illustrations that capture something of the restless night, we have included images of work by all of the artists in the exhibition. A major feature of the publication, these are sequenced with the intention of taking the reader on a nocturnal journey to the outer extremes. We hope that this book will be your night guide.

## NOTES

1 Murray Melbin, *Night as Frontier: colonizing the world after dark*, The Free Press/ Macmillan, New York, 1987, p123.

2 'Ninety percent of Gen Y surveyed worldwide said they check their smartphones for updates in email, texts and social media sites, often before they get out of bed, according to the 2012 Cisco® Connected World Technology Report (CCWTR.)', http://newsroom.cisco.com/release/1114955. Accessed 2/5/13.

Bryan Biggs is Artistic Director at the Bluecoat

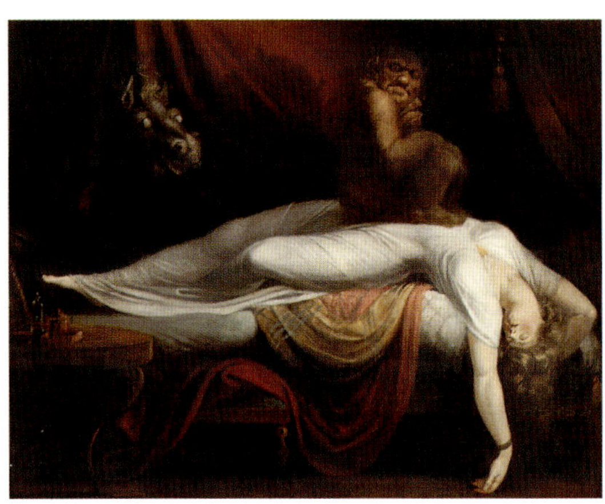

Henry Fuseli (Füssli, Johann Heinrich)
(1741–1825),
*The Nightmare*, 1781
Oil on canvas
Detroit Institute of Arts, USA,
Founders Society purchase with Mr
and Mrs Bert L. Smokler and Mr and
Mrs Lawrence A. Fleischman funds,
The Bridgeman Art Library

# CURATING THE EXHIBITION

## *3am: wonder, paranoia and the restless night*

Angela Kingston

The exhibition *3am: wonder, paranoia and the restless night* focuses on works by artists who push into night's farthest reaches, who grapple with a darker and more distant nocturnal reality. Their drawings, paintings, photographs, sculptures, films and videos are about states of mind that are folded into darkness, with many angles, shapes and textures in the folds.

I've come across writers who have, likewise, conjectured the far night as something extraordinary. For the philosopher Maurice Blanchot it is a paradox that he expresses in riddles, here in terms of life and death: '*In* the night one can die; we reach oblivion. But this *other* night is the death no one dies, the forgetfulness which gets forgotten. In the heart of oblivion it is memory without rest'.[1] For him, night's far reaches are 'an alterity located outside and beyond the succession of day and night that structures our everyday reality'.[2]

Breathtaking though Blanchot's writing is, it does not require a philosopher to describe this other kind of night. Researching the exhibition, a short phrase kept recurring, found in day-to-day conversation, on radio and TV, in newspapers, and in the writings of novelists, poets and songwriters. We refer, everywhere, to 3 a.m. – and by this hour we tend to mean, in shorthand, at some level however subtle, something quite strange and yet specific.

'The mudslide suddenly came at 3 a.m. It was so unfair, coming at that time, when people are at their most defenceless' (a Brazilian interviewed on the World Service, January 2011); the scandal of the unpaid London Olympics stewards who were turfed off their bus at 3 a.m. and told to shelter under a bridge, reported widely in the media, July 2012; '3 a.m. is the best time for skipping, when squatters raid supermarket bins' (Richard Madeley on *This Morning*, ITV, 6 December 2012); '3 a.m. is a known time for suicides' (talking with a social worker); 'I was wide awake at 3 a.m.' (friends/colleagues/self). In each case, the simple mention of 3 a.m. tips us further towards sympathy, or outrage, or dread.

It's also true that 3 a.m. exists as a mundane reality. We cross through its timeline once every twenty four hours, usually in deep slumber: 'As we sleep we whistle through the darkness, dreaming on the surface of an immense spinning top'.[3] Indeed our biology entreats us to sleep at this hour. The focus of this exhibition, on the other hand, is wakefulness and restlessness. At its outer limits it touches on semi-sleep and somnambulism. But there is no 'ordinary' sleep or dreaming. It's about a distinct reality as touched upon by artists.

In this essay, I suggest what we might learn about this 'other night' through a discussion of artworks by the twenty two artists selected for the *3am* exhibition, each of whom immediately identified with the theme. I also refer to writings, fictional and factual, that probe this hour of the night. But it is a psychic site and remains in many ways unknowable.

As much of the art attests, the night is significantly a time that belongs to the young. In **Anthony Goicolea**'s video, *Sleepers*, a camera is trained on a lamp-lit cul-de-sac, into which figures in colourful sleeping bags roll and wriggle, before disappearing just as inexplicably. In another video, *Code*, set in a wood, torch-beams pierce the darkness, casting excitedly around, and suggesting an exuberant, shared adventure. The artworks conjure with the uncommon excitement of the sleepless sleepovers and camps of late childhood and early adolescence, in which new ways of being can be tried out, unsupervised.

In **Michael Palm** and **Willi Dorner**'s video *Body Trail*, young people run in packs through city streets at night. Intermittently, we see them attaching themselves at angles to lampposts with gravity-defying poise, or piled up, one on top of the other, in phone boxes and at street corners, sometimes like corpses, at other times in elegant heaps. They have taken ownership of the city: running silent, mocking danger, sharing menace.

Sociologist Murray Melbin writes, 'The stillness of late hours appeals especially to young people, who come to feel that they possess the streets … [Teenagers] will keep late hours away with friends to avoid dominating or questioning parents. They try to dodge disputes and being nagged …'[4] To feel their imprint on the world, albeit within the anonymity of the crowd, the young go out of phase. To avoid the strictures of the daylight hours, they are drawn into the night. They have much to do, at every level; they must experiment, have their freedoms.

**Tom Wood**'s photographs of nightlife in 1980s New Brighton, across the river from Liverpool, depict young people in a club, in the final stretches of their night out. The women are mostly dressed to the nines, with their hair extravagantly preened. But the night has been long, and the poise of both the men and the women is starting to slip: eyelids are heavy, and faces are vacant and trance-like. It is a primal moment, time to clinch the deal, to see who you can get off with. Some are sidelined while others are deep in embrace.

**Sophy Rickett**'s series of photographs, *Pissing Women*, depicts young women urinating in dark city streets – while standing up. This gesture signals release from prohibition, heady freedom: they are pissing on patriarchy. This artwork has its fun, too, with tut-tuttings in the media about young women clubbers' behaviour, the scandal that they can behave as badly as men. But as a strange inflection on this, the women in the photographs appear perfectly sober, and wear smart, uncrumpled clothes.

When tiredness encroaches, when the imagination flags, drugs come to the rescue. The 3 a.m. moment, that particular state of mind, is caught and held to wonder, and stretched and magnified. **Fred**

**Tomaselli**'s *Portrait of Jim* is a night sky in which stars have been named after over-the-counter drugs and illegal stimulants taken by his subject, Jim. Caffeine, Novocaine, LSD – here's a personality, a cosmos, conjectured in terms of chemical input, headaches and highs. The stars are luminous, space is infinite, every comfort and emotion possible.

On the other hand, there are those who work at night, unseen among the revellers and part of the industry that sustains the whole delusion. In **Paul Rooney**'s sound work *Lights Go On*, a nightclub cloakroom attendant expresses the tedium of dealing with clubbers' stuck zips, lost property, queue-jumping, and emotional demands. Her words have been set to music, a catchy but deadpan, sung liturgy. The artwork builds towards the moment, at 3 a.m. – 'the very end of the night' – when the music stops and the lights go on, and crushing ordinariness re-establishes itself.

Equally, the night is for loners. **Hirsch Perlman** spent many nights in secret, up on the roof of his apartment building in Los Angeles, railing against the world and its warmongers during the war with Iraq, and building makeshift rockets and other gizmos as a gesture of defiance. He then took photographs of the rooftop that feature him with his inventions, quite alone and unseen.

Two paintings by **Anj Smith** are of night wildernesses in which humans and other creatures have taken refuge. In *Nachträglichkeit*, a bat, a badger and other animals are safely hibernating together, suspended within a gossamer-thin fabric that is tethered to the sky. In *Post-Pastoral Secrets*, a weathered wayfarer's marker hung with talismans points to repeated journeys, on foot, into the darkness; the need for escape has become a state of being.

Here is Melbin again, this time on the night as refuge, somewhere we can 'colonise', the day being now so overcrowded: '… conquest of the darkness opens a new zone capable of meeting people's needs for escape and opportunity … Persons who are disparaged or oppressed retreat to its tolerant atmosphere … Night's hush and solitude attract people looking for a haven from stress'.[5]

But look again and 3 a.m. contains its very opposite. It's a world in extremis, with pressures untold. **Dorothy Cross**'s diptych of photographs, *Searchlight*, depicts a helicopter search for someone lost in the ocean. Quite utterly lost, in the infinite darkness, in the vast waters of the sea. Heedless, or suicidal, or abjectly unlucky, quite possibly already dead: who can say if he or she can be brought back to the day? Hope consists of a beam of light, trained on the sea by another human being, only just perceptible in the darkness.

In the night's far reaches, we witness the extremities of humanity: utter helplessness and the untold tenderness of a person intent on rescue. Something of this commingling of need and generosity, borne of the very dead of night, is found in an incident described by F. A. Worsley in *Shackleton's Boat Journey*. Having not slept for days, the author has been steering a tiny, leaking boat, with only an awning for cover, in a relentless Antarctic storm:

> Between 3 and 4 A.M. [the first officer] found that I was cramped by wet and cold. I had been steering in a constrained position, sitting on the stores, for twenty hours. As he seized the tiller, I said, 'Let me know when you close the land.' As Macklin and McLeod put me under the dripping folds of the tent, I asked them to straighten me out and rub my thighs and groins. While they did this – straightening me out like opening a jackknife – I fell fast asleep in their hands. After they had vigorously massaged my stomach and legs they lay, one on each side, under the tent to keep some of the breaking seas off me.[6]

**Jordan Baseman**'s video *A Nasty Piece of Stuff* introduces still other extremes of human behaviour, as a man tells the story of how once, working into the small hours, he went out into the streets of London for some air, and was raped. The horror continues with the discovery that he has contracted gonorrhoea, and with the scorn of the medic who treats him. As a visual counterpoint to the incredulous, and remarkably steady, tones of the narrator, are rapid, staccato sequences of the night – the camera swaying wildly, the screen streaked with neon. These visuals – the sense of them breaking down – serve on the one hand to express the distress that the man remains numb to, and on the other, the violence of the perpetrator.

The writings of Charles Dickens are strongly associated with the night, particularly its far depths: 'that time which … may be truly called the dead of night, when the streets are silent and deserted, when even sound appears to slumber and profligacy and riot have staggered home to dream.' In *Oliver Twist* the action pivots around an attempted house-burglary at a time approaching 3 a.m. Under the cover of darkness Fagin's criminal gang is in its element, while poor Oliver, forced to take part, is 'well nigh mad with grief and terror'.[7] We hear also of the panic of the servants of the house, but to comic effect this time. Here, again, different facets of humanity converge around a single event in the dead of night.

If the night can make us feel all-powerful, then sometimes this has negative consequences (as with Fagin's gang). As reported by the *Daily Mail*, night nurse Anne Grigg-Booth 'believed she was in control of the rules after dark', allegedly administering lethal doses of painkilling drugs to up to twenty patients. The article continues: 'at night on the quiet wards, the matron – "utterly convinced of her own clinical prowess" – believed she carried ultimate authority'.[8]

Something of this megalomania infuses **Nathan Mabry's** sculpture *Eat Your Heart Out*, of a clean-cut boy with a hideous, grimacing, monster riding on his shoulders. Rendered in blackened metal, this impossible pairing is a shadow, a dark apparition, a child who has turned his worst fears to his advantage, a monster made more monstrous. Each dons one of a pair of boxing gloves and boxing boots, and they are ready for anything.

**Danny Treacy** seeks out the occupants of the urban night via the soiled clothes he finds in side streets, alleys and graveyards, and by lock-up garages. To him, these places are 'fertile grounds, where the human animal reveals itself.' Against all instinct, he dresses up in those clothes and creates life-size self-portrait photographs that confront us with nightmarish personas: a man-pig in malevolent velveteen; a hospital reject survivalist; a night-worker automaton. In each photograph in this series, titled *Them,* he becomes the bogeyman, a shape-shifting embodiment of dread.

Drawings by **Marc Hulson** conjure with what the dark corners of our own homes conceal. It's much as William Herbert, seventeenth-century writer of religious tracts, put it: 'The night is more quiet, then the day: and yet we feare in it what we doe not regard by day. A Mouse running, a Board cracking, a dog howling, an Owle scritching put us often in a cold sweat'.[9] Hulson sets the scene with *dramatis personae* that could be taken for a family. But he also brings to the stage a clawed monster in human clothing, a grotesque, reptilian eye, and another eye that weeps and dissolves. And there is a drawing of a staircase – that oftentimes most frightening of places, with inexplicable shadows and creakings. I am reminded of other nocturnal invasions of domestic spaces, as envisaged by eighteenth century artists: Fuseli's *The Nightmare*, a demonic figure squatting on a deeply slumbering woman, and Goya's *The Sleep of Reason Produces Monsters*, a sleeping man mobbed by owls, bats and cats (pages 02:10 and 02:06).

In contrast to these perceptions of a 3 a.m. 'dread zone', there are artworks that engage with how the distant night is also wholesale cessation, quietness and *in*activity, the lifting of the pressures of the day. As the globe turns and darkness falls, the nocturnal hours bring respite and repose, as night cleanses day.

**Bettina von Zwehl** wrested people from their beds in the middle of the night, at the deepest point of sleep. She made them face her camera, individually, to have their portraits taken. Mentally, her subjects seem entirely elsewhere; physically, they appear barely able to hold themselves. The fact that they wear white against a white background renders them almost ethereal: night inundates them, flushing out the day's dirt and debris.

I was surprised when a whole section of the exhibition turned out to be bright and white. But then I heard about a French phrase *nuit blanche*, or 'white night', meaning a night without sleep. Its origins are in the middle ages, when knights prayed all night, dressed in white, purifying themselves before battle.

**Tonico Lemos Auad**'s sculpture *Sleepwalkers* is comprised of curiously shaped white lace orbs hanging from the ceiling, lit internally. They are part 1960s lampshade, part fleeting-glimpse-of-nightie, part floating dream-bubble (the nocturnal equivalent of a thought-bubble). The delicate humour of this artwork connects with the weightlessness that night can bring. The day is purged and all is whiteness.

**Ed Pien**'s *Spectral Drawings* are drawn with white ink on black paper. The surfaces teem with half-human figures that grin or grimace or stare. Floating in the darkness, many have coagulated into groups. Some seem to perform ritualistic gestures; they appear to be flailing, waving, turning. The white marks are in many places broken and smudged, the figures sometimes barely there. Pien's phantom-creatures seem to rise and fall, advance and recede – 'without weight, without bones, without body'.[10]

In **Rachel Kneebone**'s white porcelain sculptures, there are tangles of limbs and bodies that dissolve into one another, and individuals with pod-like upper bodies. Noticeably, there are no heads: all is lost to sensation. In *Study in self-sufficiency II*, the foot of a supine feminine figure on a funerary pedestal arcs with sexual urgency. Both sexual and deathly, Kneebone's sculptures are redolent of Blanchot's vision of the '*other* night' as a 'death no one dies': they are distant night's most alien workings.[11]

As we travel still further into the night, thoughts expand outwards. On a clear night, there's the sensation of a lurch upwards, too: there's no roof on the world; stars thousands of light years away are visible.

**Sandra Cinto** compulsively creates drawings of the night sky. Often working in white ink, chalk, or pencil, she covers entire walls with images of individual stars, whole galaxies, and also strangely floating boulders. She frequently draws rope ladders, suspended precariously from who-knows-where, suggesting a desire to travel further still. Sometimes the drawings are loosely layered over each other, hinting at universe after unknown universe. Pencil-probe in hand, the artist reaches out beyond all limits, ever further into the night – at one with her drawing, mere matter in the cosmos.

The night is also nature's own time: for hunting, feeding, mating and the care of young. Most creatures in the wild are primarily active at night.[12] With our poor night vision and limited sense of smell, humans are mere interlopers. Curious as to what her dogs were barking at during the night, **Dornith Doherty** placed motion-activated cameras around her suburban Texan home. She'd glimpsed coyotes by day, but was surprised by how many prowl at night, a time she describes as 'teeming with secret life', when deer, armadillos, possums, raccoons and bobcats were also observed. Revealingly, the creatures are barely captured by the camera: their fleeting forms sleek across the picture plane, their eyes blur with movement and light.

**Lucy Reynolds** filmed a lake in a London park at night. She opened her camera shutter for three seconds per frame of celluloid, allowing enough time for an image to imprint itself. As a consequence, the camera reveals far more than was visible to the eye, while everything also appears speeded up, creating a hyperreal landscape of uncanny twitchings and rustlings and flows. Water birds skitter feverishly across the lake's surface and bushes shudder as if made of flesh. It is as travel writer Robert Macfarlane has described: night utterly changes the senses, producing a new awareness of the very substance of a landscape, and creating a strange fusion of past and present.[13]

In *Nightwatch*, a video by **Francis Alÿs**, a fox is let loose in the National Portrait Gallery in London at night, and filmed by CCTV cameras as it roams from room to room. The fox ambles past rows of masterpieces in the richly decorated rooms, eventually finding an ornate table on which to curl up. The video contrasts two extremes: nature embodied in the fox; culture epitomised by the museum. It raises the question of what a museum *is* when there are no humans to populate it and give it meaning. Night and nature are seen to re-define terms, rendering a museum of high culture into a kind of wilderness.

On and on and through and through. At 3 a.m., there's doubt that the day will ever come: time is looped, or repeats, or eats its own tail. The mind falters and slides, and ideas come that would not otherwise. It is for this reason that the far night state *belongs* to artists. Art needs the strangeness of 3 a.m. and its utter loneliness, too, to force the hand, to reach the 'why not?' state. The exhibition *3 am: wonder, paranoia and the restless night* drips with insomnia. It needs to keep different hours. It is an adolescent running free, a man alone and afraid, a woman gazing at the cosmos, an unexpected coupling, an emboldened fox.

NOTES

1 Maurice Blanchot, *The Space of Literature*, first published in 1955; University of Nabraska, 1989, trans. Ann Smock, p. 164.
2 Elizabeth Bronfen on Blanchot, in 'The Powers of Insomnia', in *Louise Bourgeois: The Insomnia Drawings*, ed. Peter Fischer, DAROS, Zurich, 2000, p. 37.
3 Christopher Dewdney, *Acquainted with the night*, Bloomsbury, London, 2004, p. 33.
4 Murray Melbin, *Night as Frontier: colonizing the world after dark*, The Free Press/ Macmillan, New York, 1987, pp. 59–60.
5 *ibid.*, pp. 36–7.
6 F. A. Worsley, *Shackleton's Boat Journey*, about the ill-fated expedition to the Antarctic in 1914–16, first published in 1940; Pimlico, London, 1999, p. 81.
7 Charles Dickens, *Oliver Twist*, first published in 1838; Wordsworth, Herefordshire, 1992, pp. 433 and 198.
8 http://www.dailymail.co.uk/news/article-1285128/Did-nurse-Anne-Grigg-Booth-kill-20-Matron-drugged-patients-ruled-wards.html, 9 June 2012, accessed 20 December 2012.
9 William Herbert, *Herbert's Devotions: or, a Companion for a Christian. Containing Meditations & Prayers, fitted for all Conditions, Persons, Times and Places. Either for the Church, Closet, Shop, Chamber, or Bed. Being reasonable and Usefull for these sad unsettled Times*, 1657, London, p. 231, *Early English Books Online*, <http://www.jischistoricbooks.ac.uk/Search/?bibnumber=Wing%20H1542&spage=1> accessed 27 February 2013. Original spellings and capitalisations have been retained.
10 From Franz Kafka's diary entry for 6 June 1912, in which he describes walking the streets of Prague at night. *The Diaries of Franz Kafka*, ed. Max Brod, trans Joseph Kresh (1910–1913 only) Penguin, 1975, p. 204.

11 3 a.m. is widely considered to be the most likely time to die. Interestingly, this is more imagined than real. See http://www.theatlantic.com/health/archive/2012/11/you-are-most-likely-to-die-at-11-am/265427/, accessed 29 January 2013.

12 This was the assertion of *The Dark: Nature's Night-time World*, a BBC Two series screened in summer 2012.

13 *The Wild Places*, Granta, London, 2008, p. 193.

Angela Kingston is a freelance curator and writer

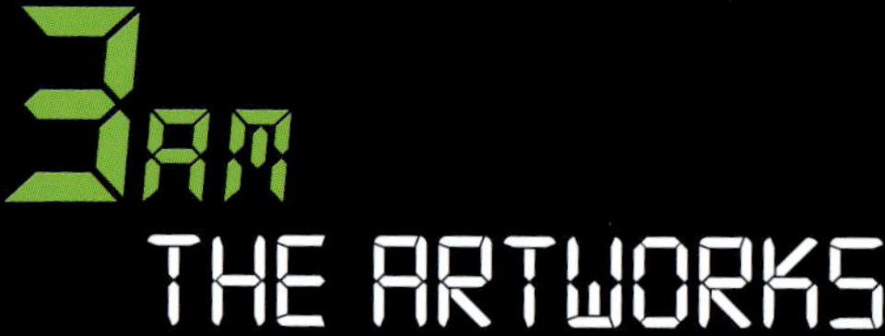
3AM
THE ARTWORKS

The following pages comprise images of works from the exhibition *3 am: wonder, paranoia and the restless night*.

Captions indicate works in order from left to right.

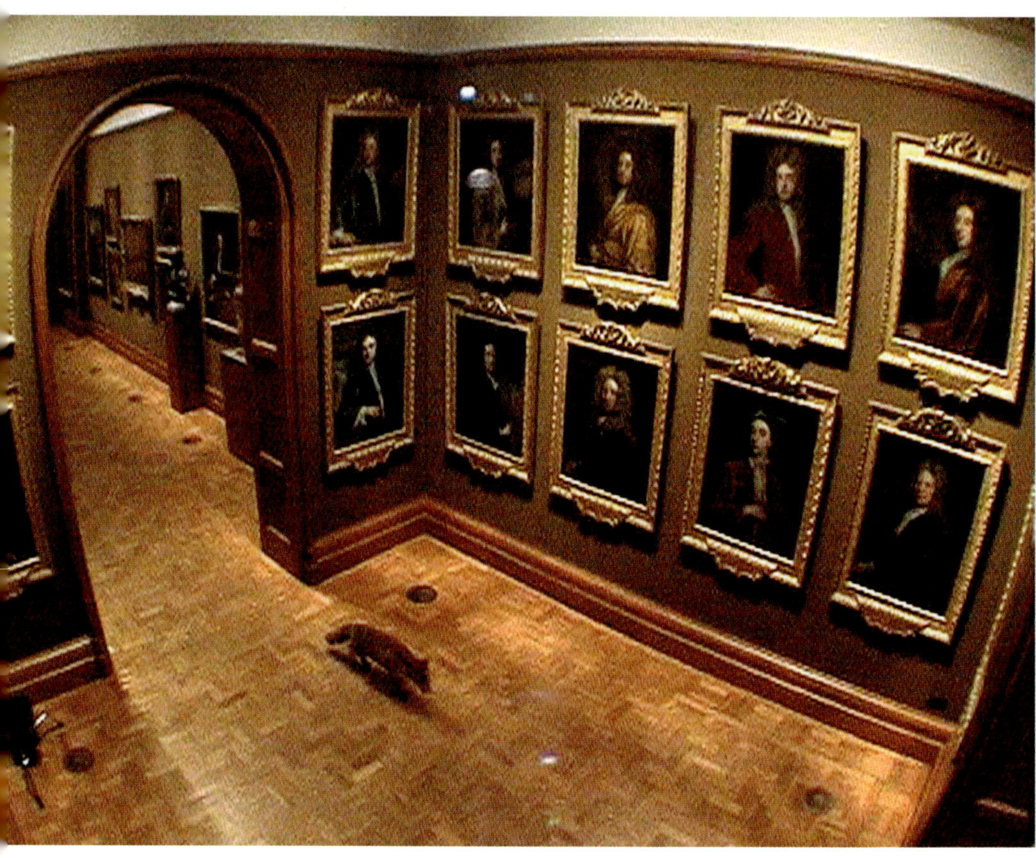

Francis Alÿs
*The Nightwatch*
London, 2004, in collaboration with Rafael Ortega and Artangel
Single-channel video on monitor; colour, silent, 17.30 minutes
Courtesy David Zwirner, New York/ London

Above: video still, opposite: detail of video still. Images include paintings in the National Portrait Gallery. Opposite: left (detail) *Queen Elizabeth I,* unknown English artist, circa 1600 (NPG 5175), and *Mary, Queen of Scots,* after Nicholas Hilliard, circa 1610 (NPG 429)

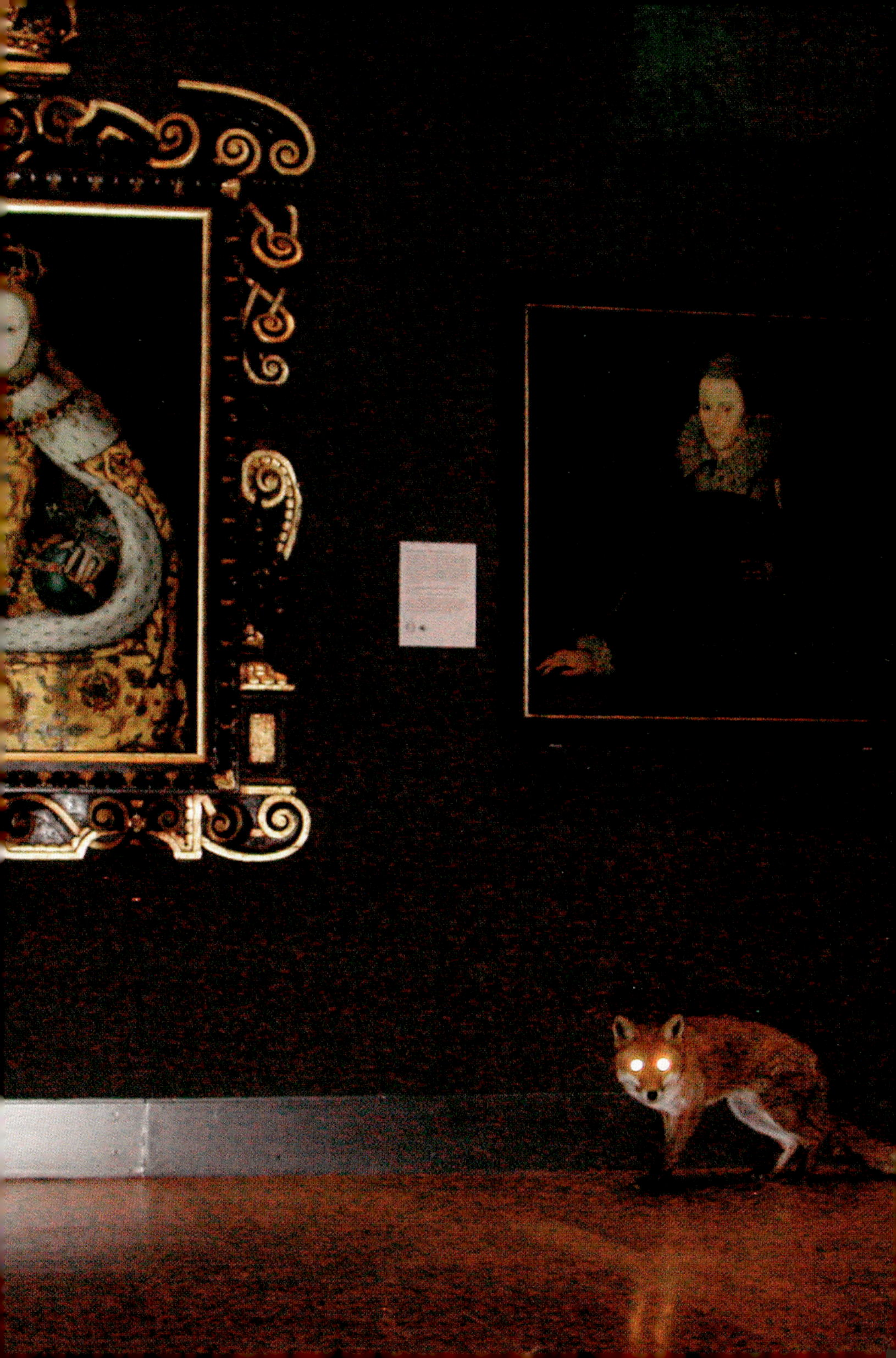

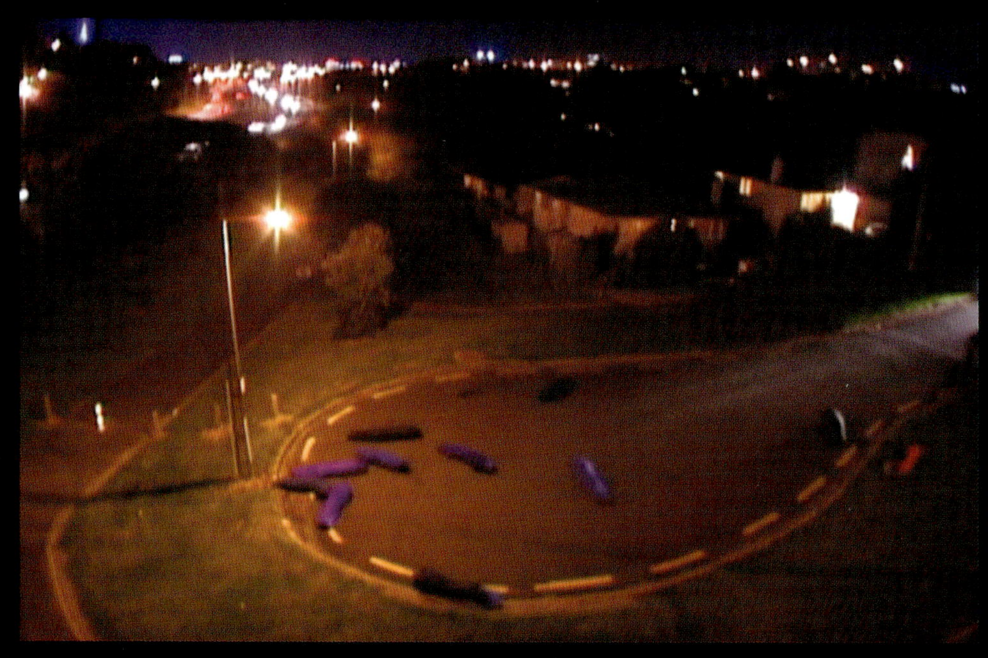

Anthony Goicolea
*Sleepers,* 2002
*Code*, 2007
Film stills from two original single channel videos, colour and sound
Courtesy of Postmasters Gallery, New York City

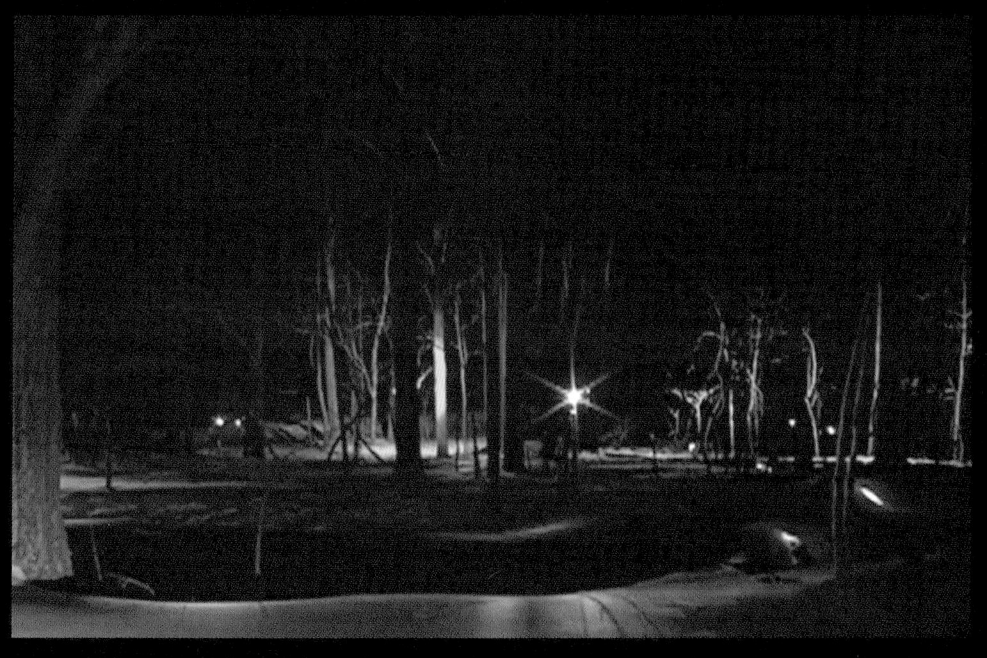

02:27

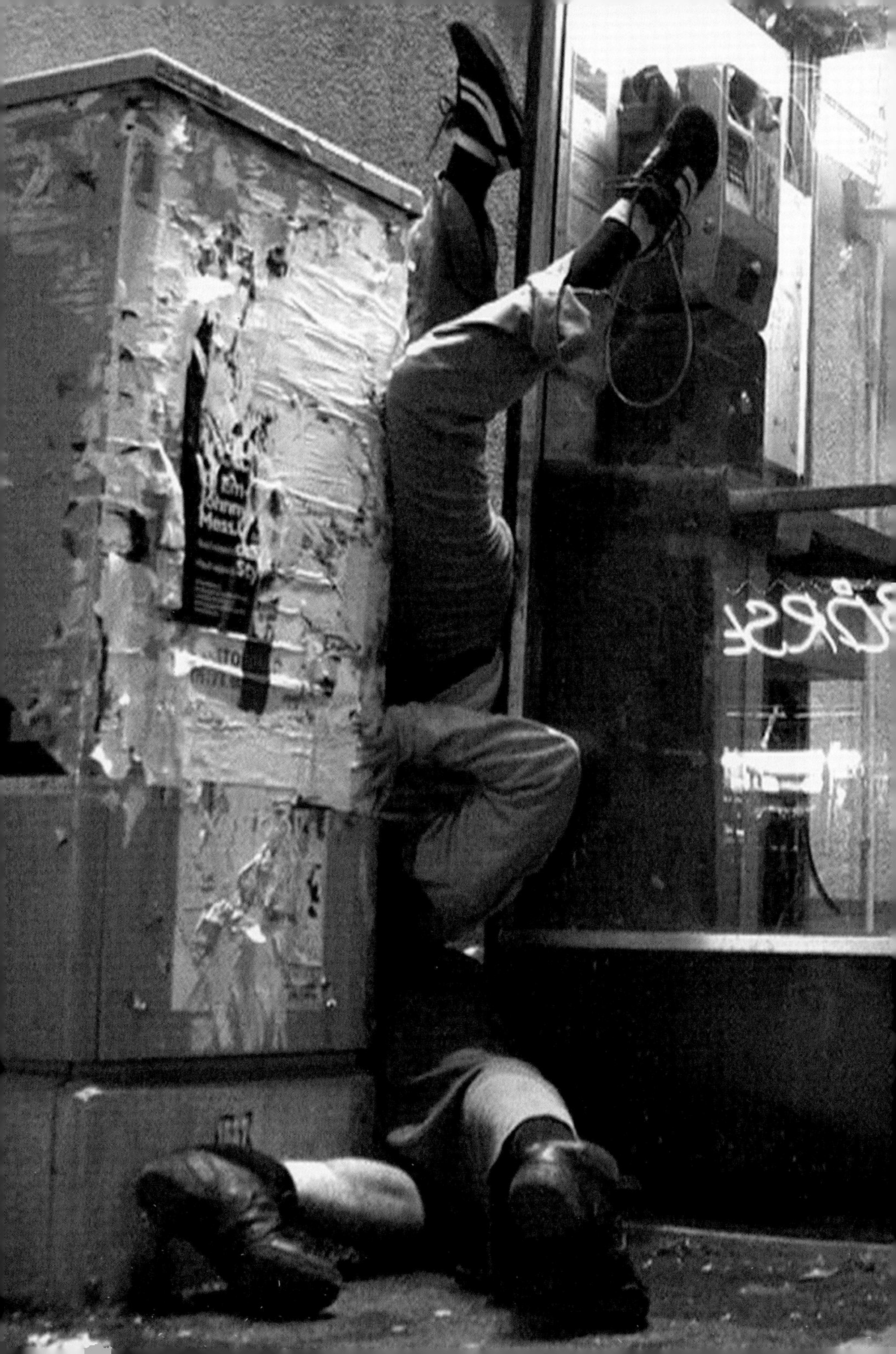

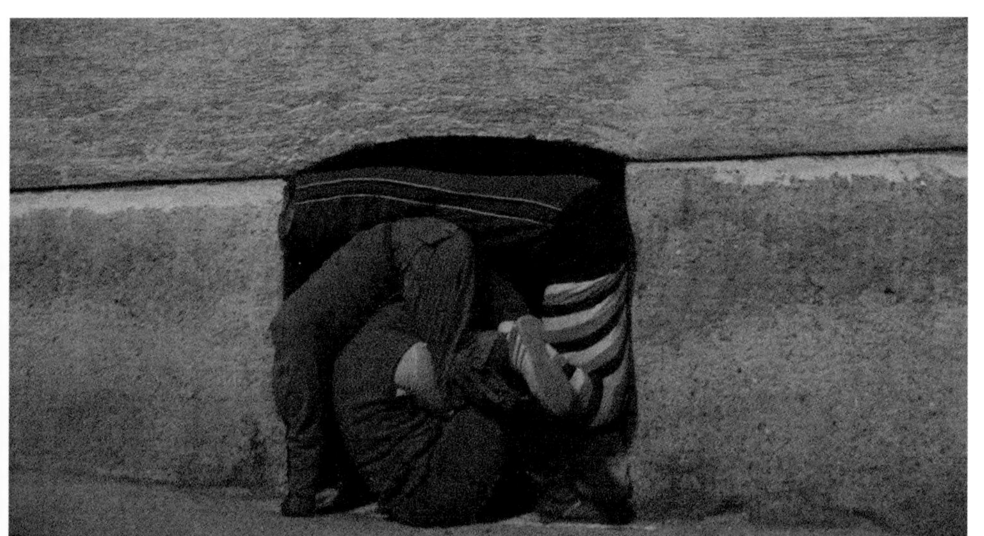

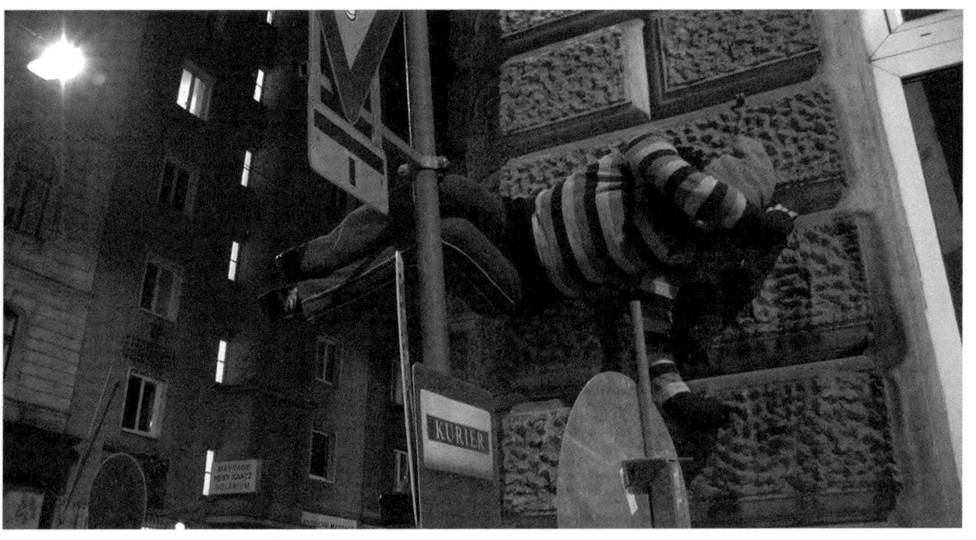


Michael Palm and Willi Dorner
*Body Trail,* 2008
Film stills from original film
Courtesy Sixpackfilm

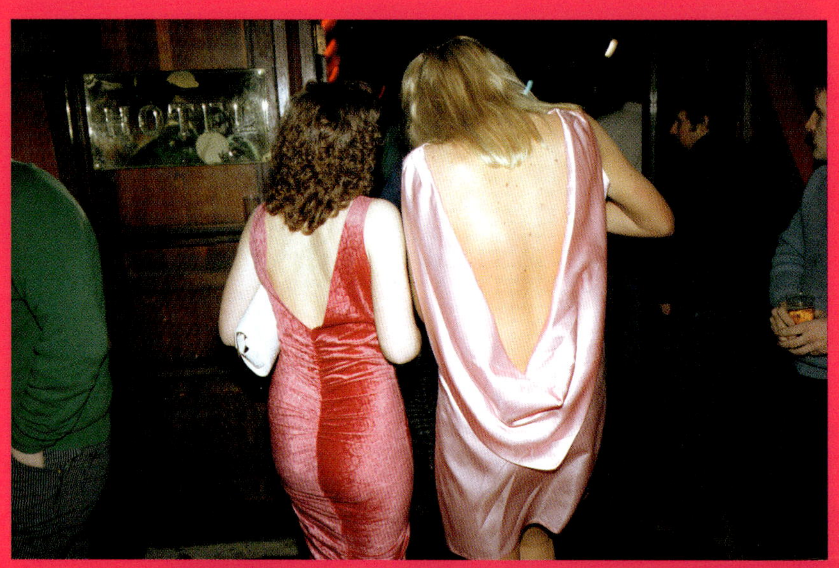


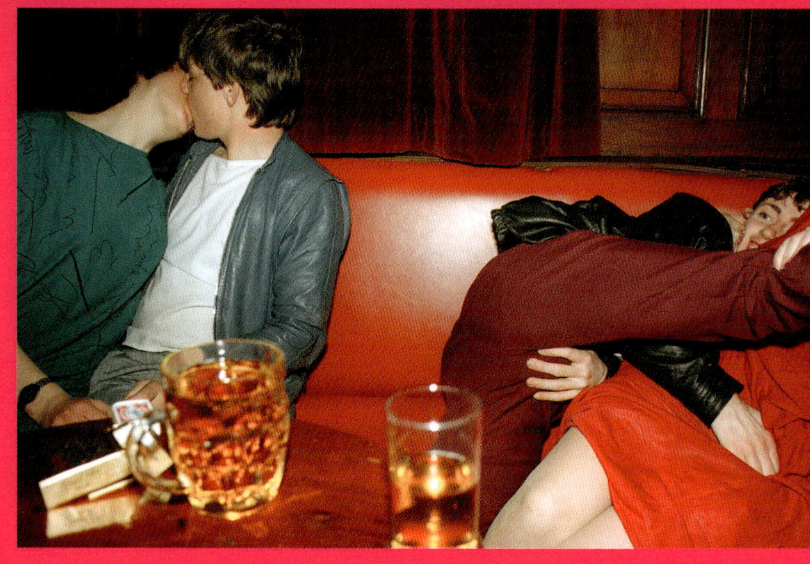

02:30

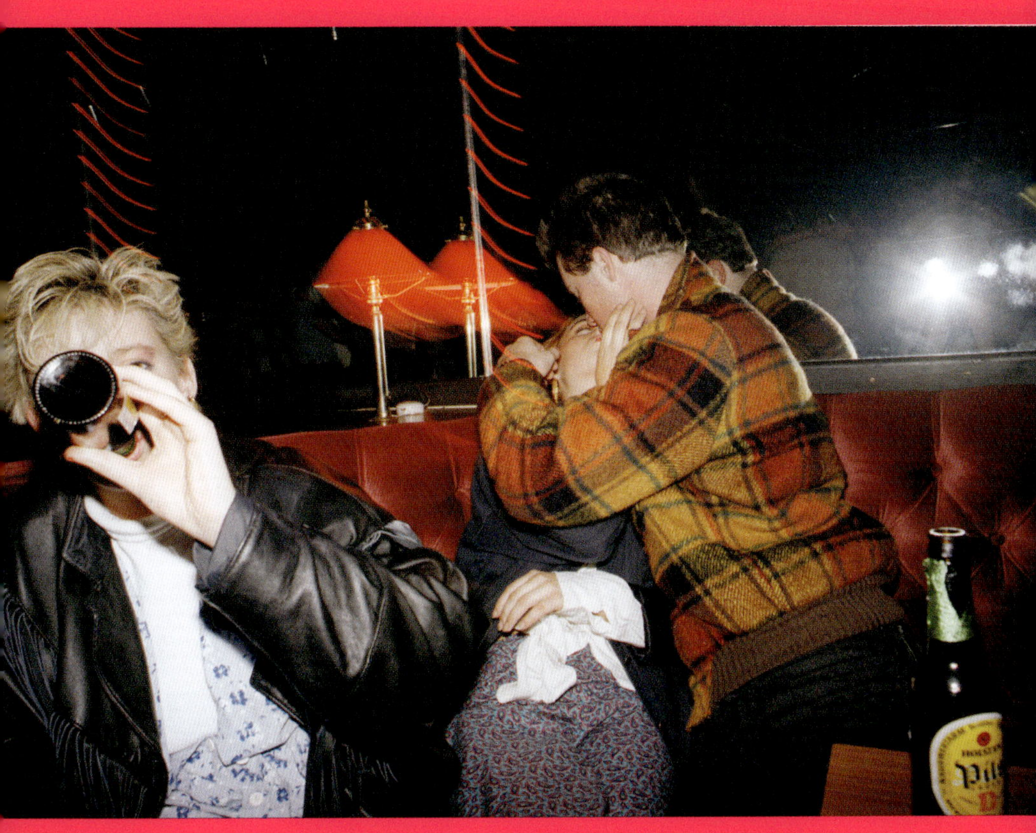

Tom Wood
from *Looking for Love* series, 1983–86
*Back Cover*, 1984
*Leg Over*, 1985
Both C-type, 47.5 × 62 cm (frame size)
*Lumberjack Kiss, 1986,*
C-type, 58 × 75 cm (frame size)
Courtesy the artist

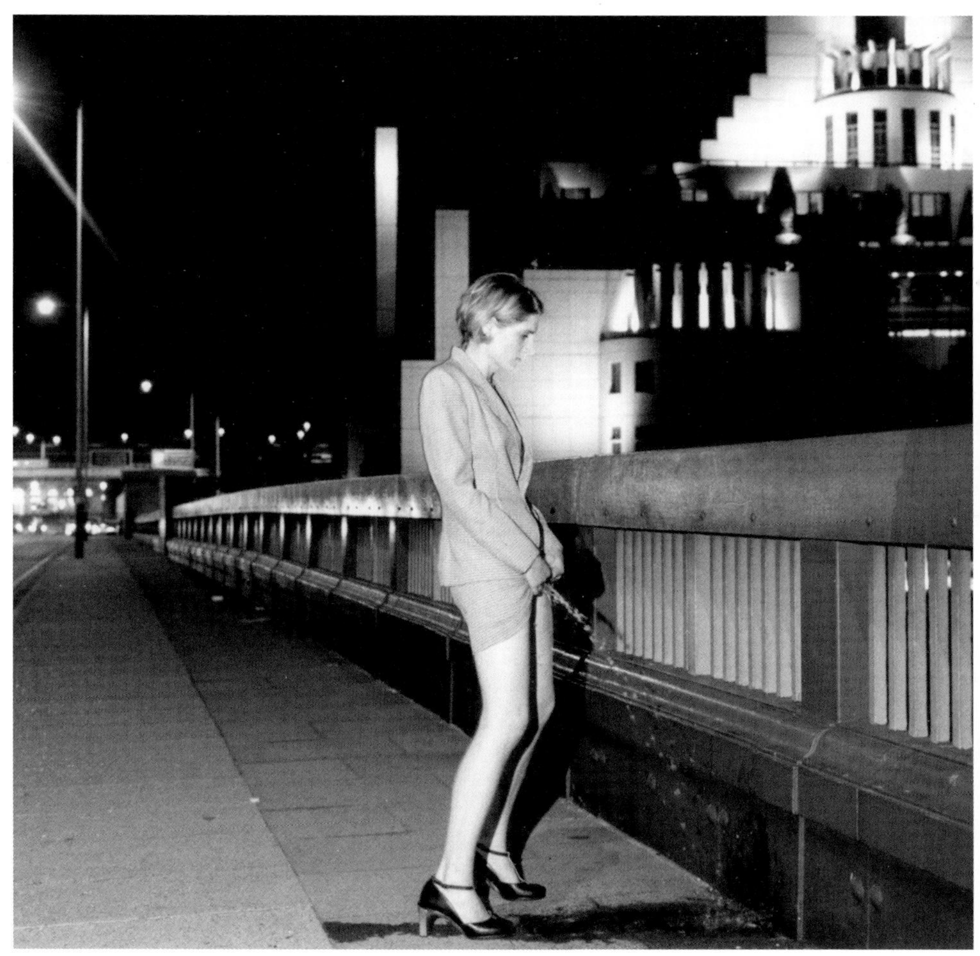

Sophy Rickett
from the series *Pissing Women*, 1995
*Vauxhall Bridge*
*Silvertown*
Gelatine silver prints
Courtesy the artist and Brancolini
Grimaldi, London

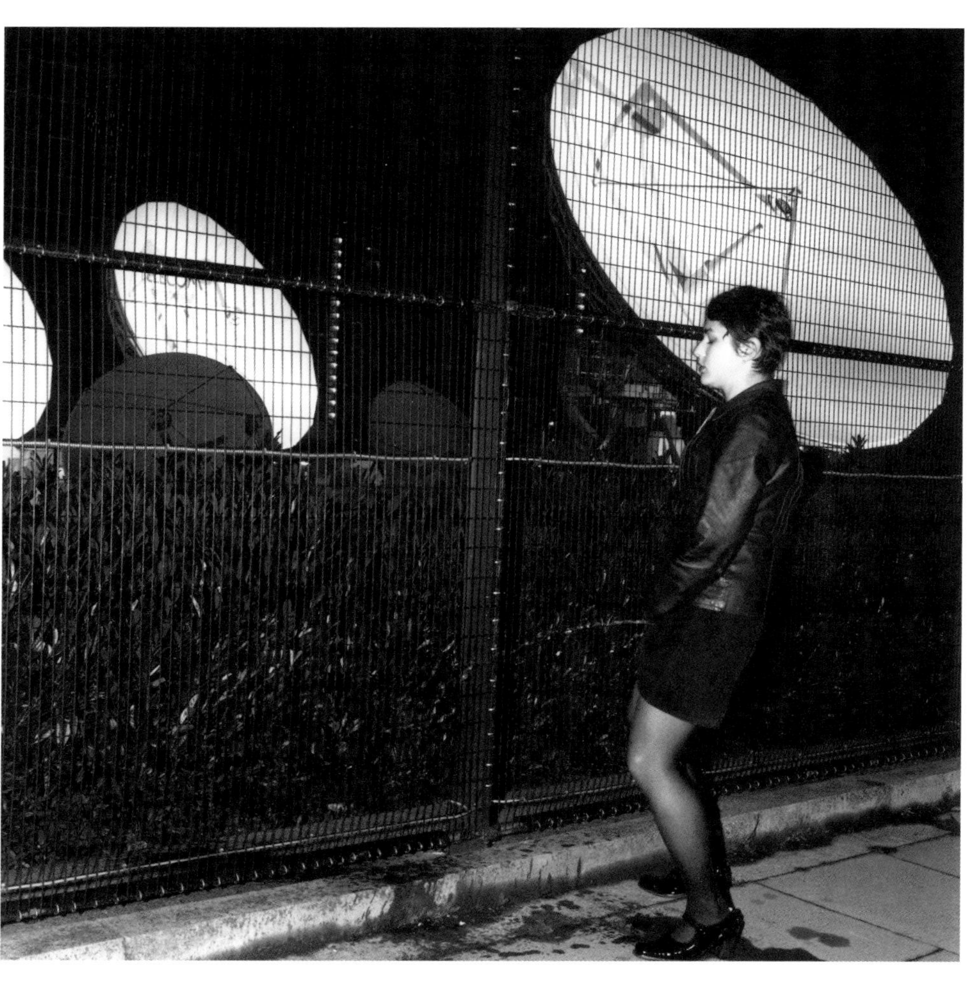

02:33

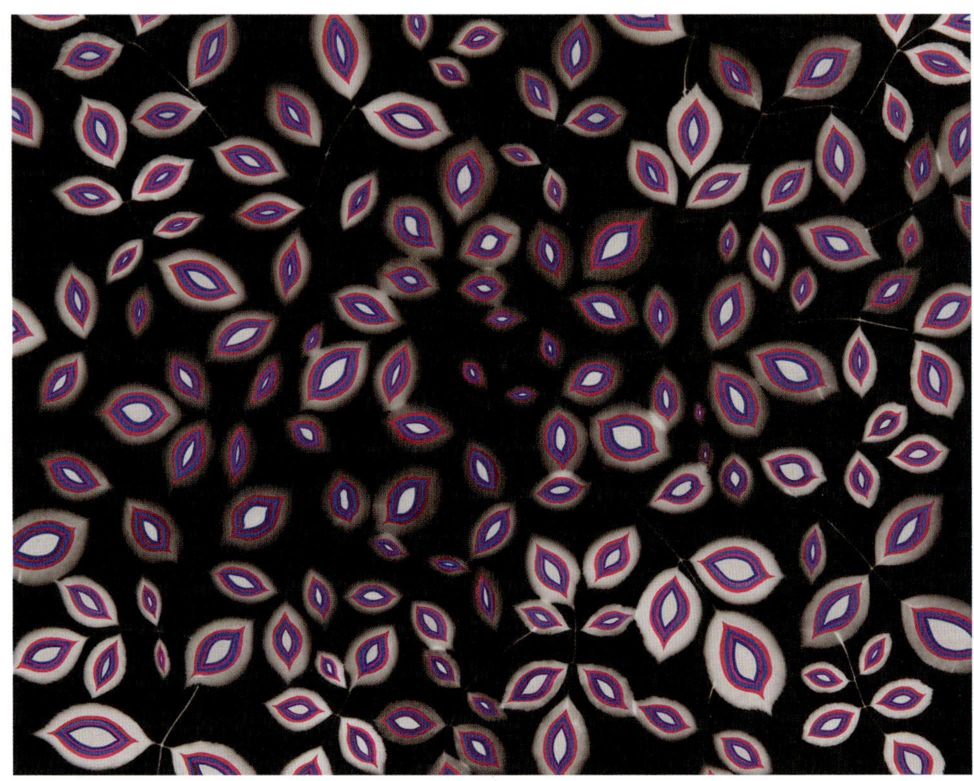

Fred Tomaselli
*Untitled*, 2012
Gouache on unique photogram,
40.6 × 50.8 cm
*Portrait of Jim,* 2012
Prismacolor on unique photogram,
40.6 × 50.8 cm

Photos: Erma Estwick (this page);
Christopher Burke (opposite)

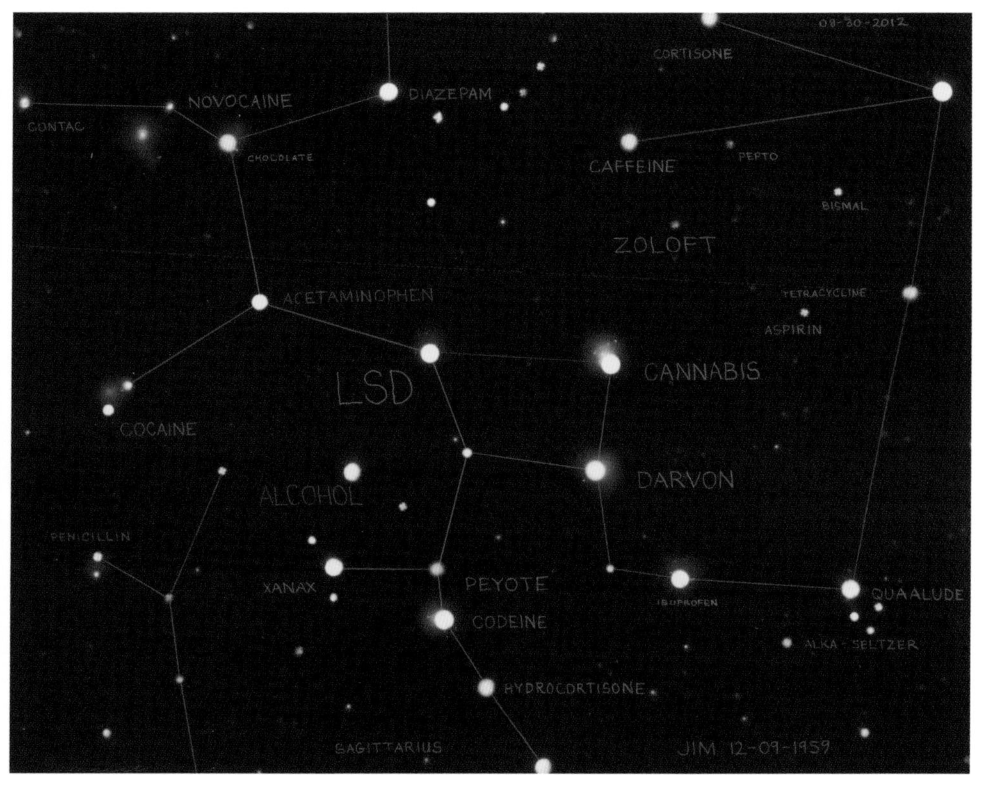
08-30-2012
CORTISONE
NOVOCAINE
DIAZEPAM
CONTAC
CHOCOLATE
CAFFEINE
PEPTO
BISMAL
ZOLOFT
ACETAMINOPHEN
TETRACYCLINE
ASPIRIN
LSD
CANNABIS
COCAINE
DARVON
ALCOHOL
PENICILLIN
XANAX
PEYOTE
CODEINE
IBUPROFEN
QUAALUDE
ALKA-SELTZER
HYDROCORTISONE
SAGITTARIUS
JIM 12-09-1959

Paul Rooney
*Lights Go On: the song of the nightclub cloakroom attendant,* 2001
(Sound only version exhibited)
Words and music Paul Rooney, adapted from a text by Melodie Hook, nightclub cloakroom attendant
Courtesy the artist

# LIGHTS GO ON

Between the hours of nine and three on Friday and Saturday nights,
inside a box with open hatch I hang and grab hats, coats and bags.
The queue begins at ten o'clock and people hurl questions at me.
I have to be a clubber's guide, it's all part of the service here.

Lights go on the very end of the night.
My tasks include sorting taxis, lost property, and fixing zips.
I am the club's agony aunt: the clubbers tell me their secrets.
Lights go on the very end of the night. Lip-stick on the teeth and
louts pushing in to the queue, full of drink, and no-one leaves any tips.

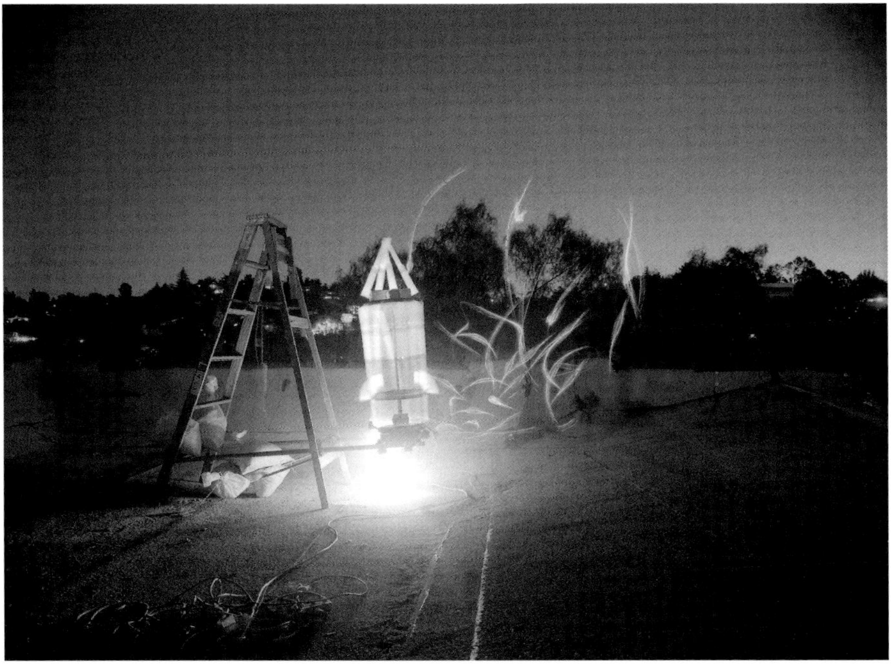

Hirsch Perlman
*Apparatum Armorum Ineptum #3*,
2003–04 (61 × 76.2 cm)
*My Reproof #11*, 2003–04
(40.6 × 50.8 cm)
*My Reproof #16,* 2003–04
(40.6 × 50.8 cm)
Gelatine silver prints
Courtesy the artist

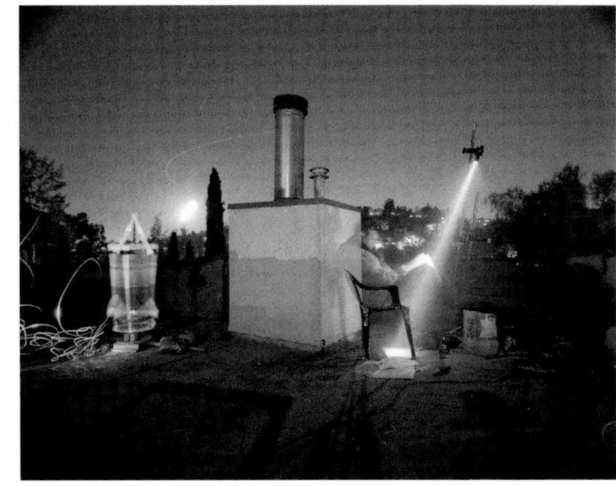

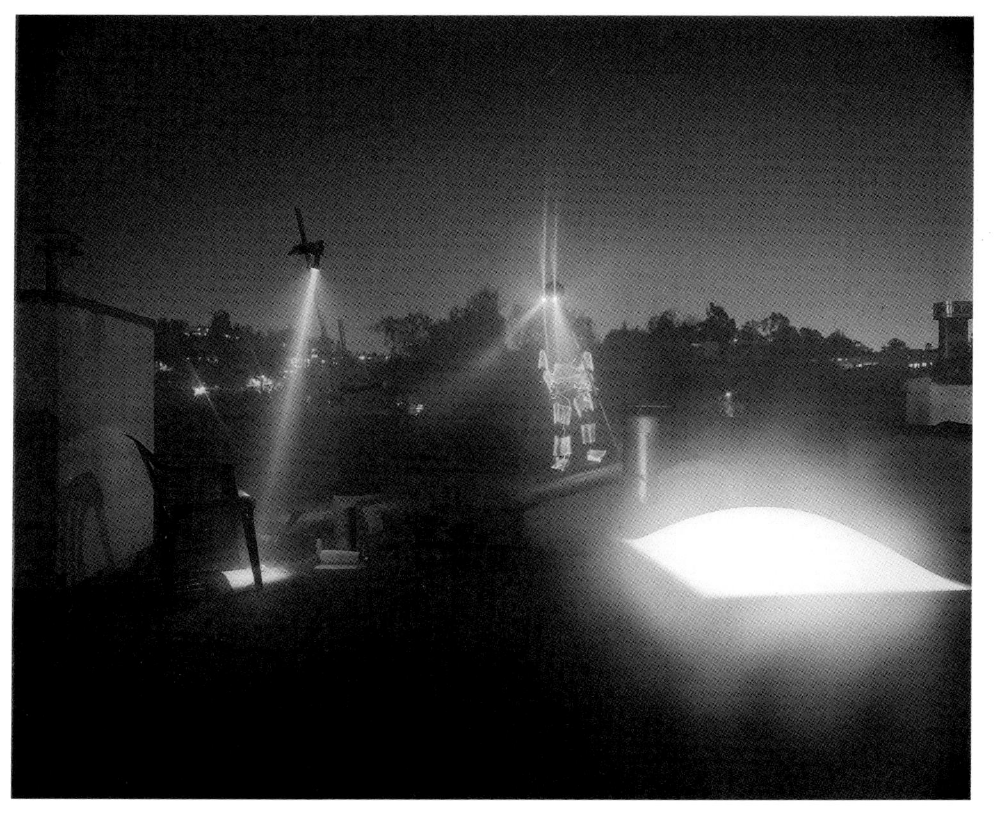

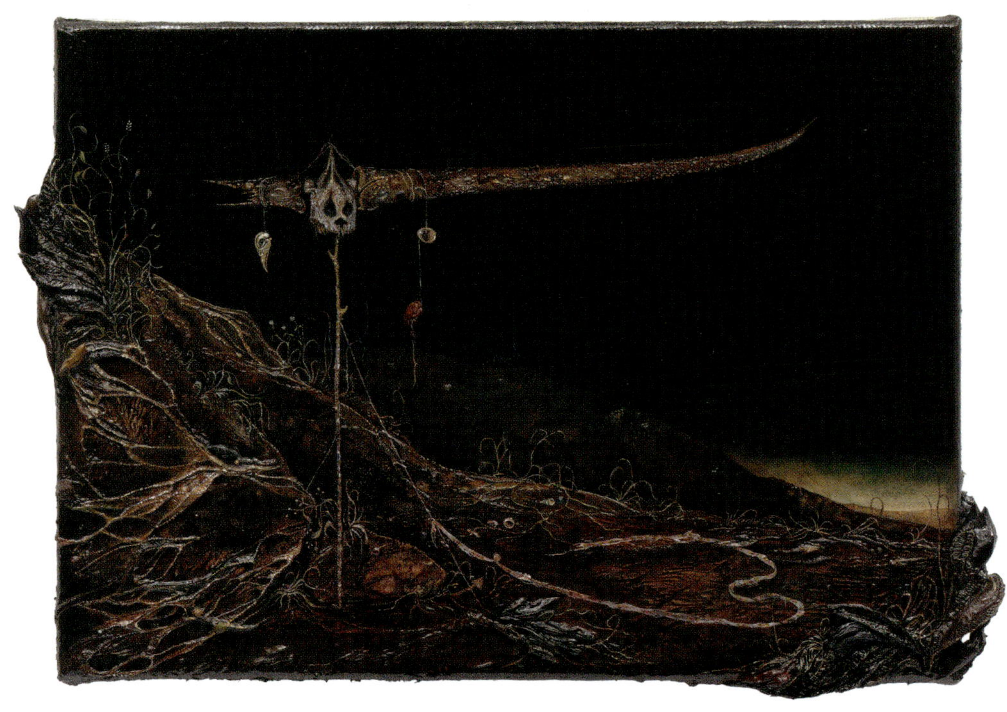

Anj Smith
*Post-Pastoral Secrets,* 2010
Oil on linen, 18.5 × 26.5 cm
Courtesy Hauser & Wirth Collection, Switzerland

*opposite*
Anj Smith
*Nachträglichkeit,* 2010
Oil on linen, 19 × 24.7 cm
Collection of Amrita Jhaveri.
Courtesy the artist and Hauser & Wirth

Photographs: Alex Delfanne

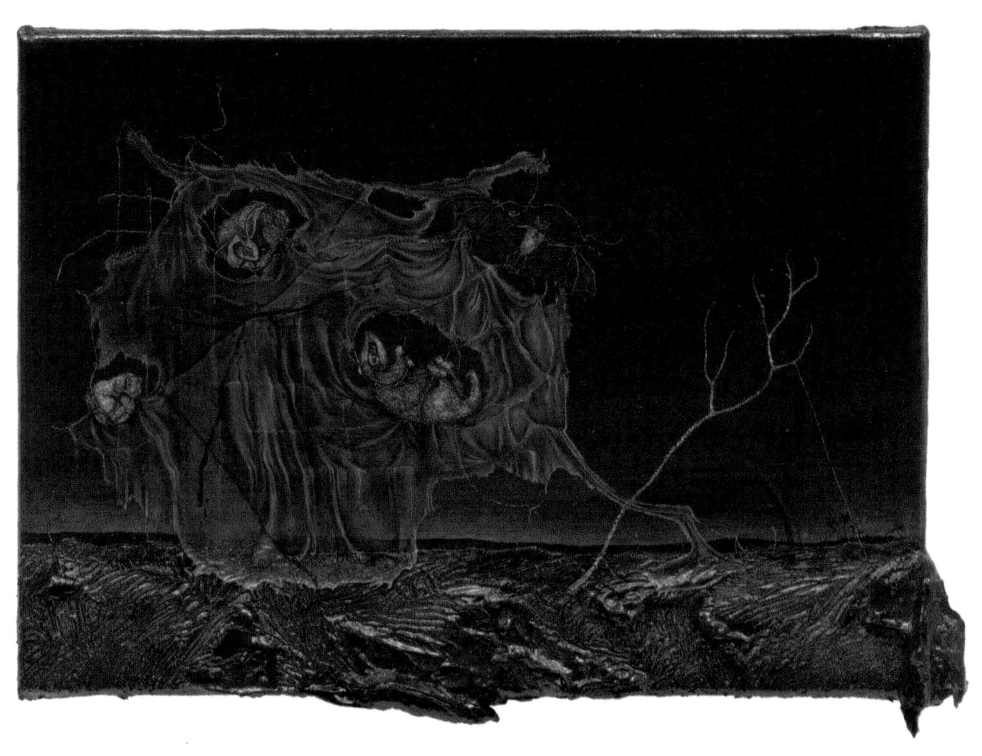

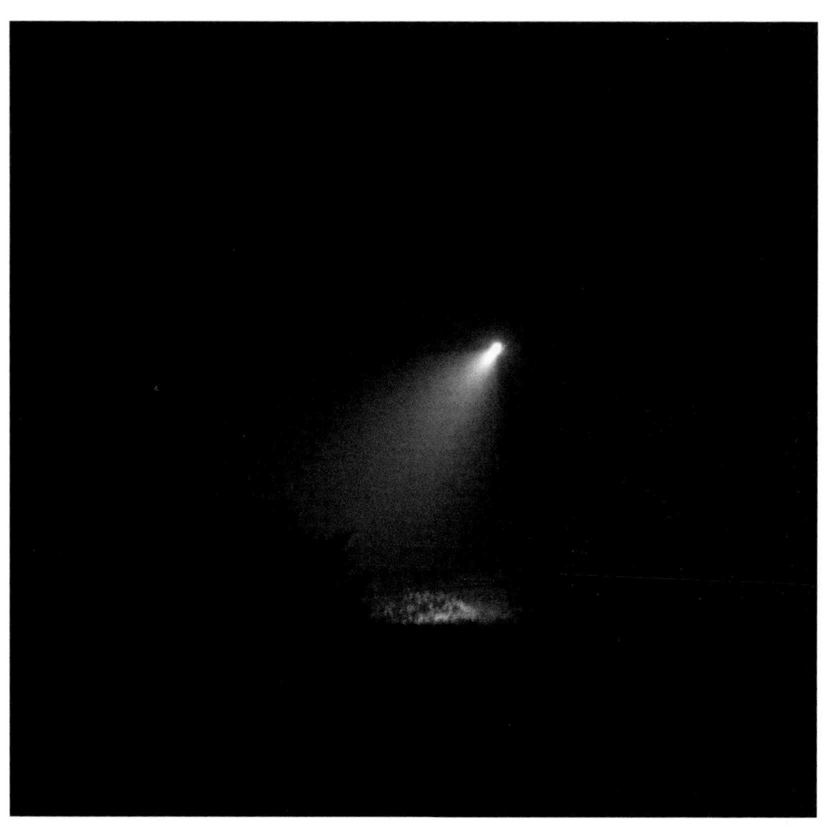

Dorothy Cross
*Searchlight*, 2008
Giclee prints on Hahnemühle photo rag paper. Diptych, 101 × 75 cm (each image)
Courtesy the artist and Frith Street Gallery

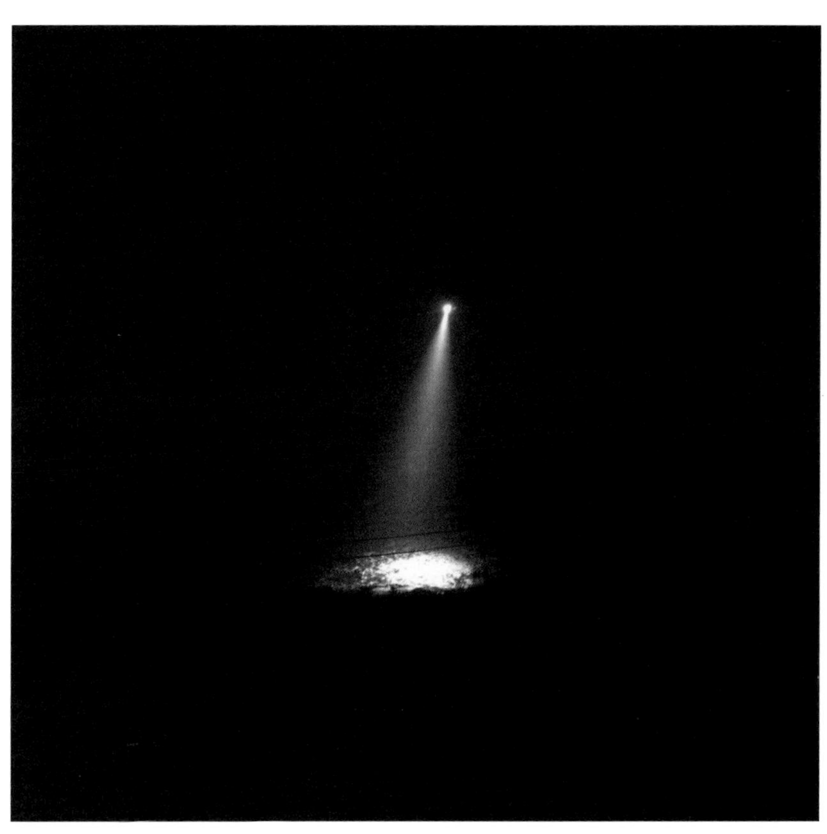

*overleaf*
Jordan Baseman
*Nasty Piece of Stuff*, 2009
Film still
Courtesy the artist and
Matt's Gallery, London

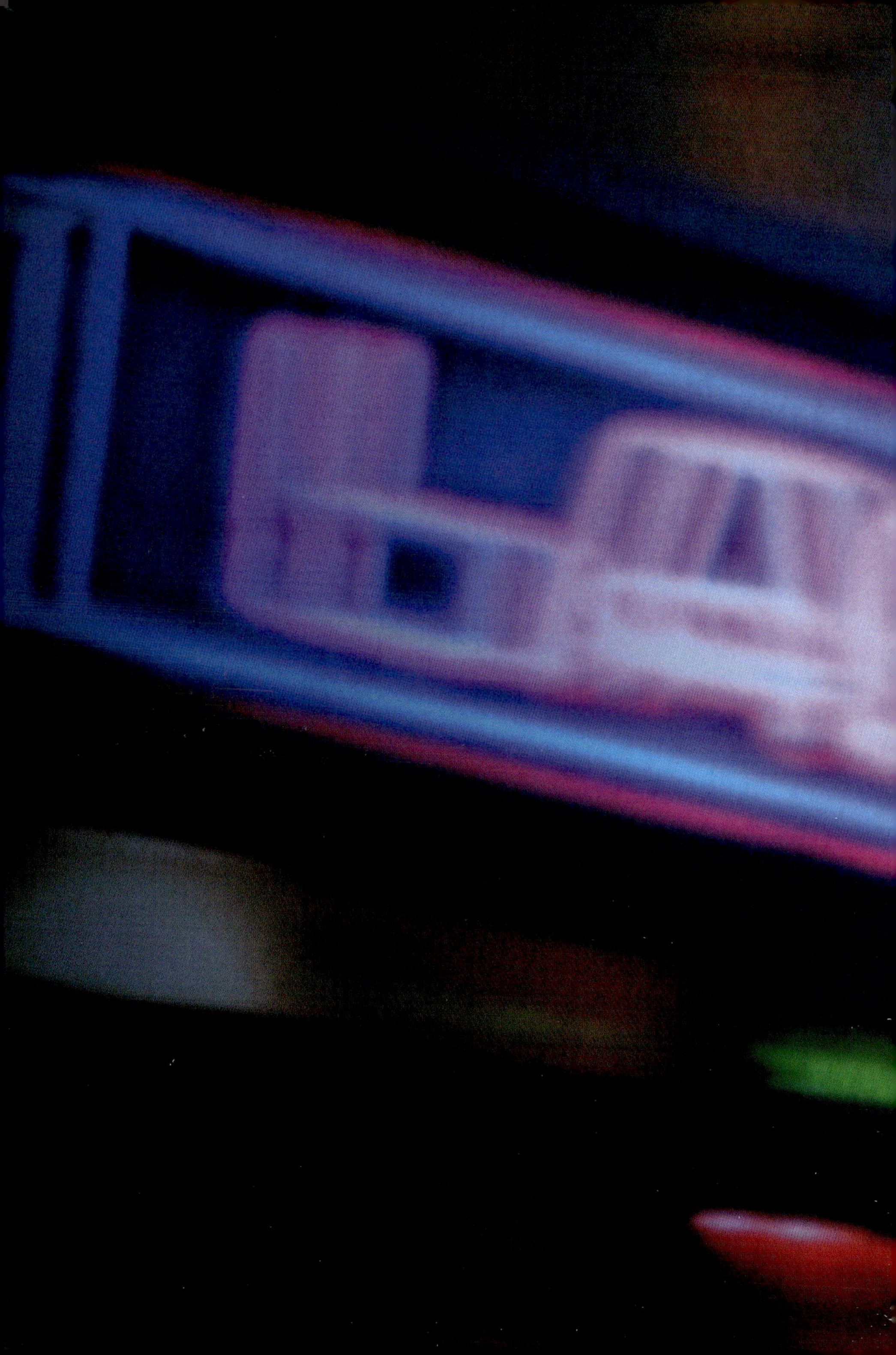

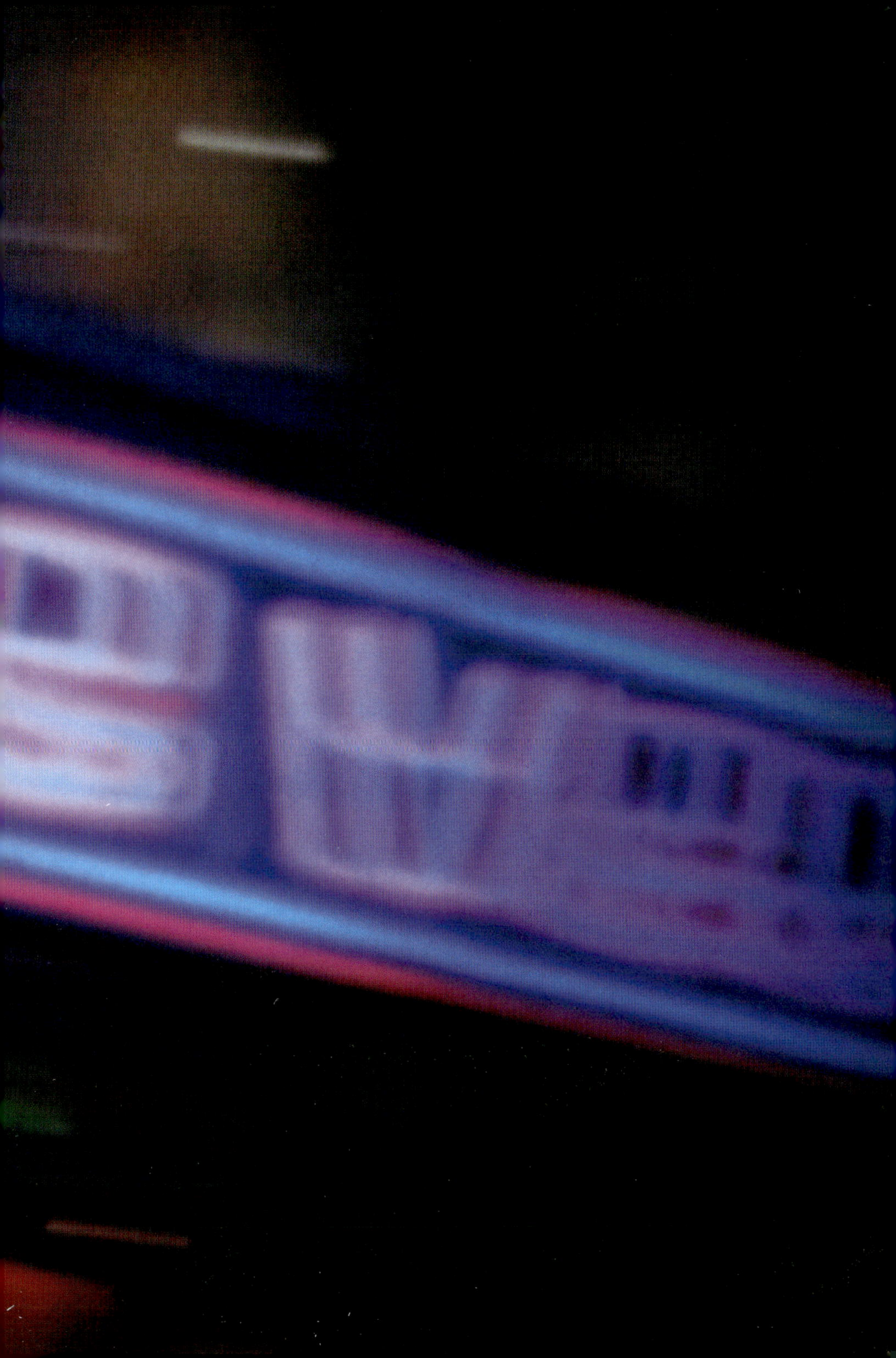

Nathan Mabry
*Process Art (Eat Your Heart Out...)*, 2007
Bronze, marble and wood,
213.36 × 91.44 × 60.96 cm
Private collection
Photo: Robert Wedemeyer

*pages 02:47–48*
Danny Treacy
*Them #15*, 2005
*Them #24*, 2010
Lambda digital C prints mounted on
aluminium, each 215 × 180 cm
Courtesy the artist

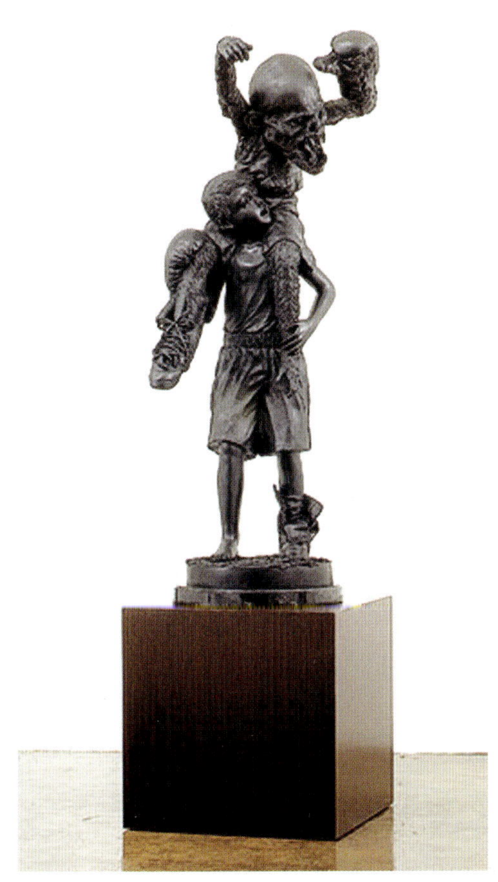

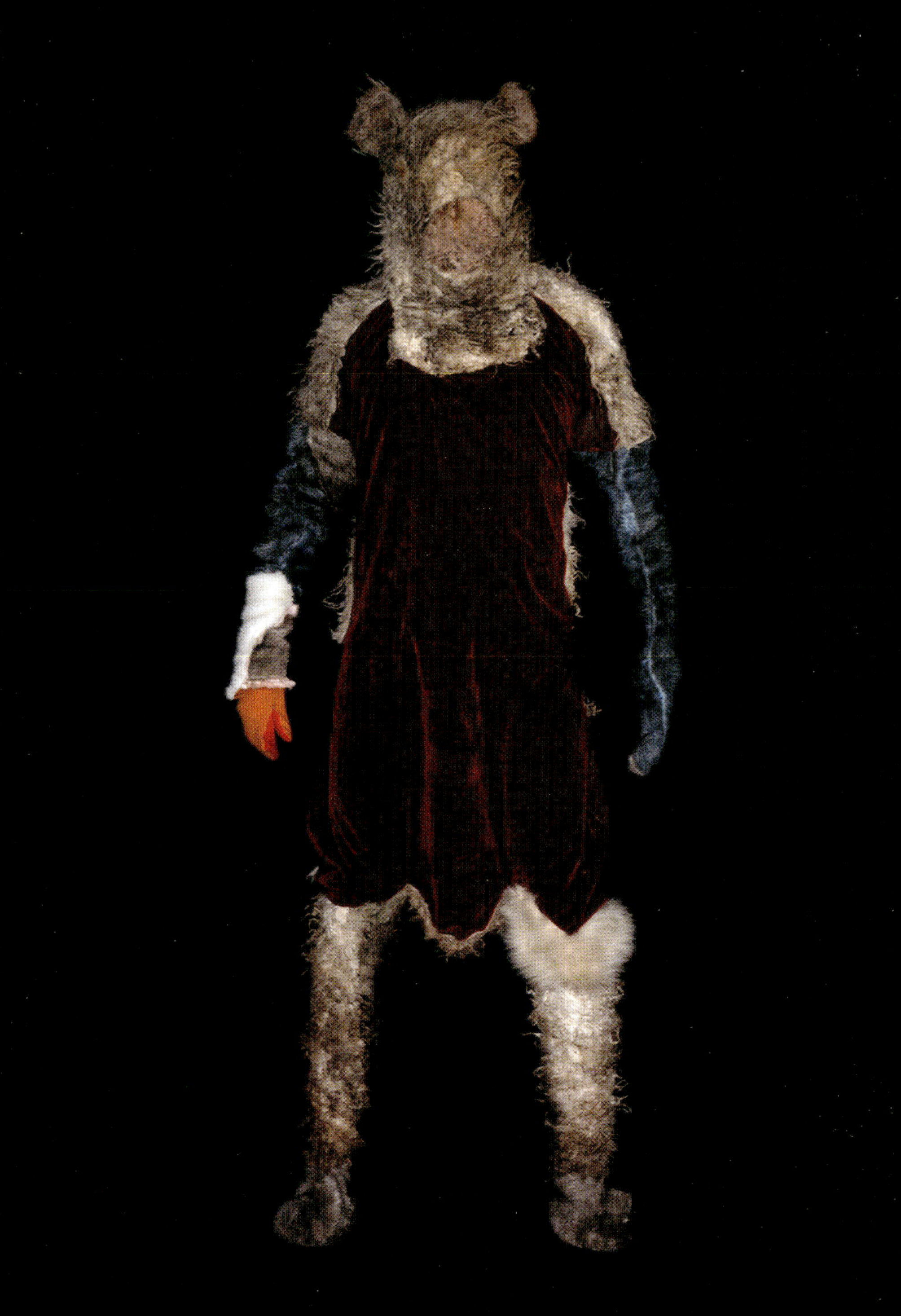

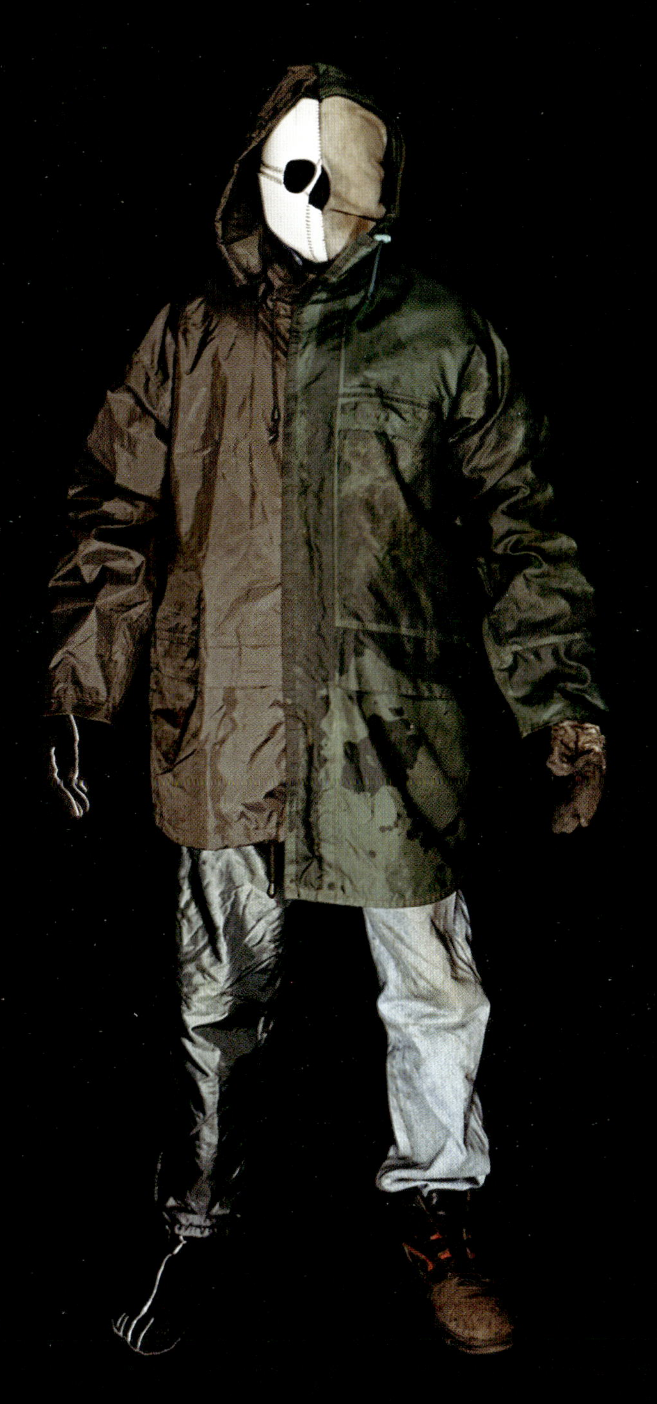

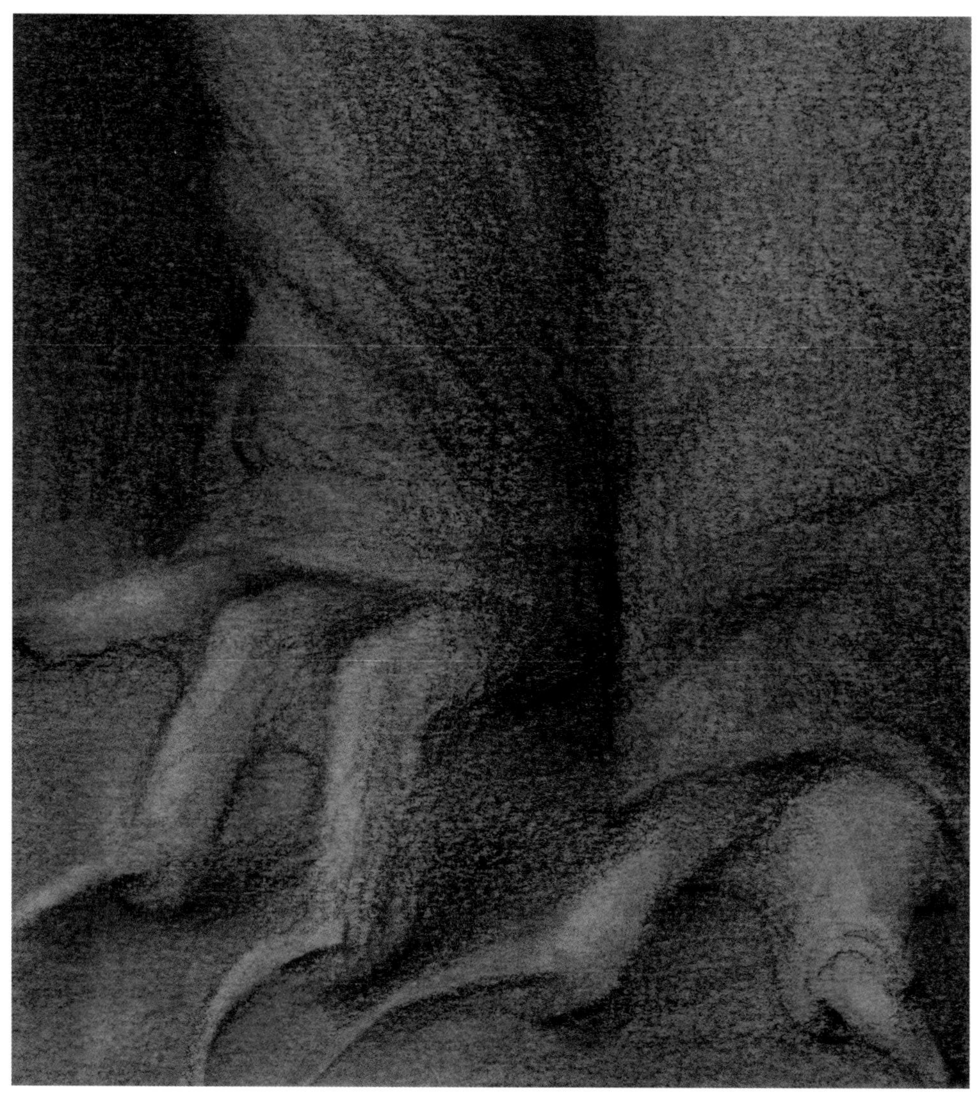

Marc Hulson
*Untitled,* 2000 (17.1 × 15 cm)
*Untitled,* 2012 (18 × 16 cm)
Graphite on paper
Courtesy the artist

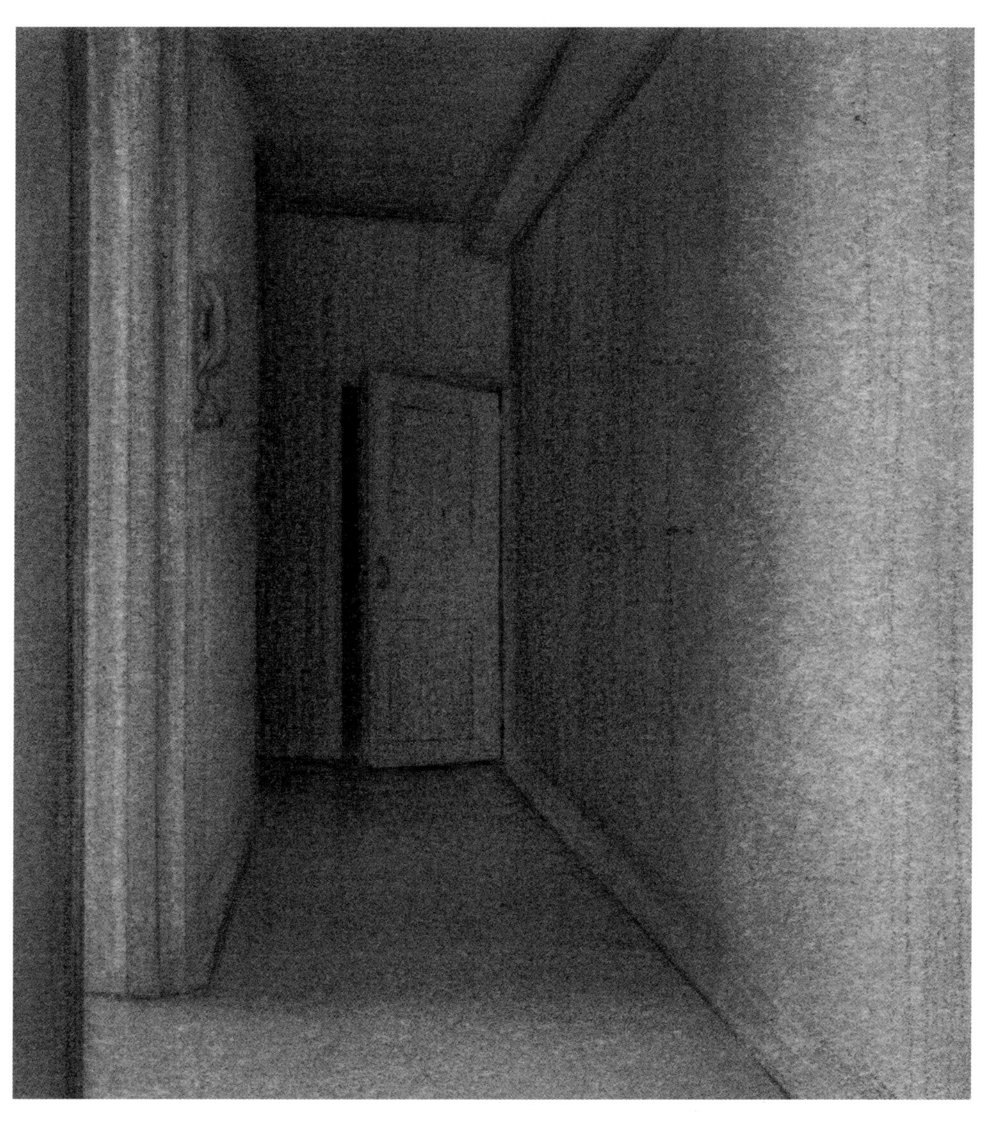

*overleaf*
Bettina von Zwehl
*Untitled I no 1*, 1998
*Untitled I no 2,* 1998
C-type prints, each 50.8 × 40.6 cm
Courtesy the artist and Purdy Hicks Gallery

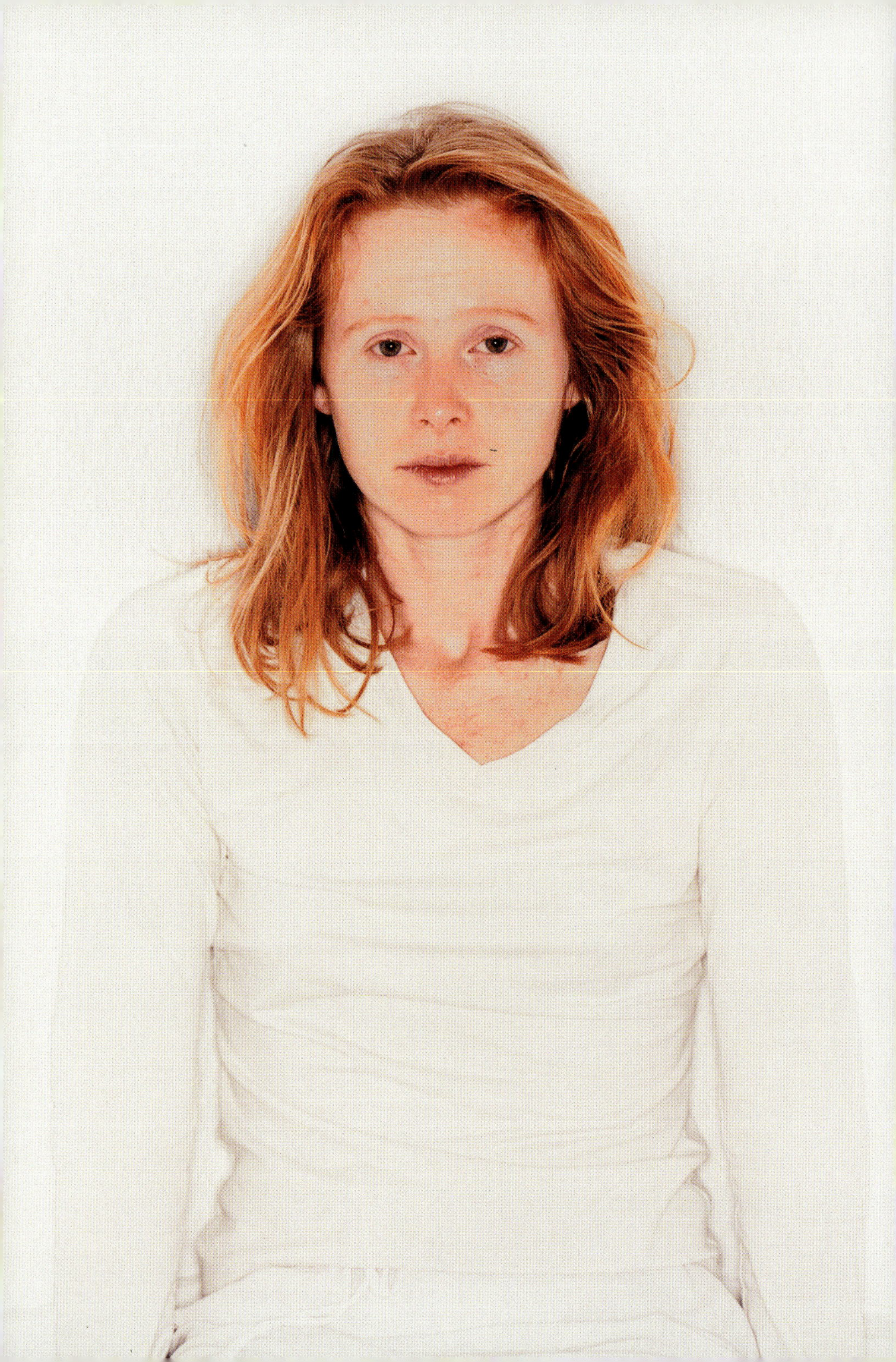

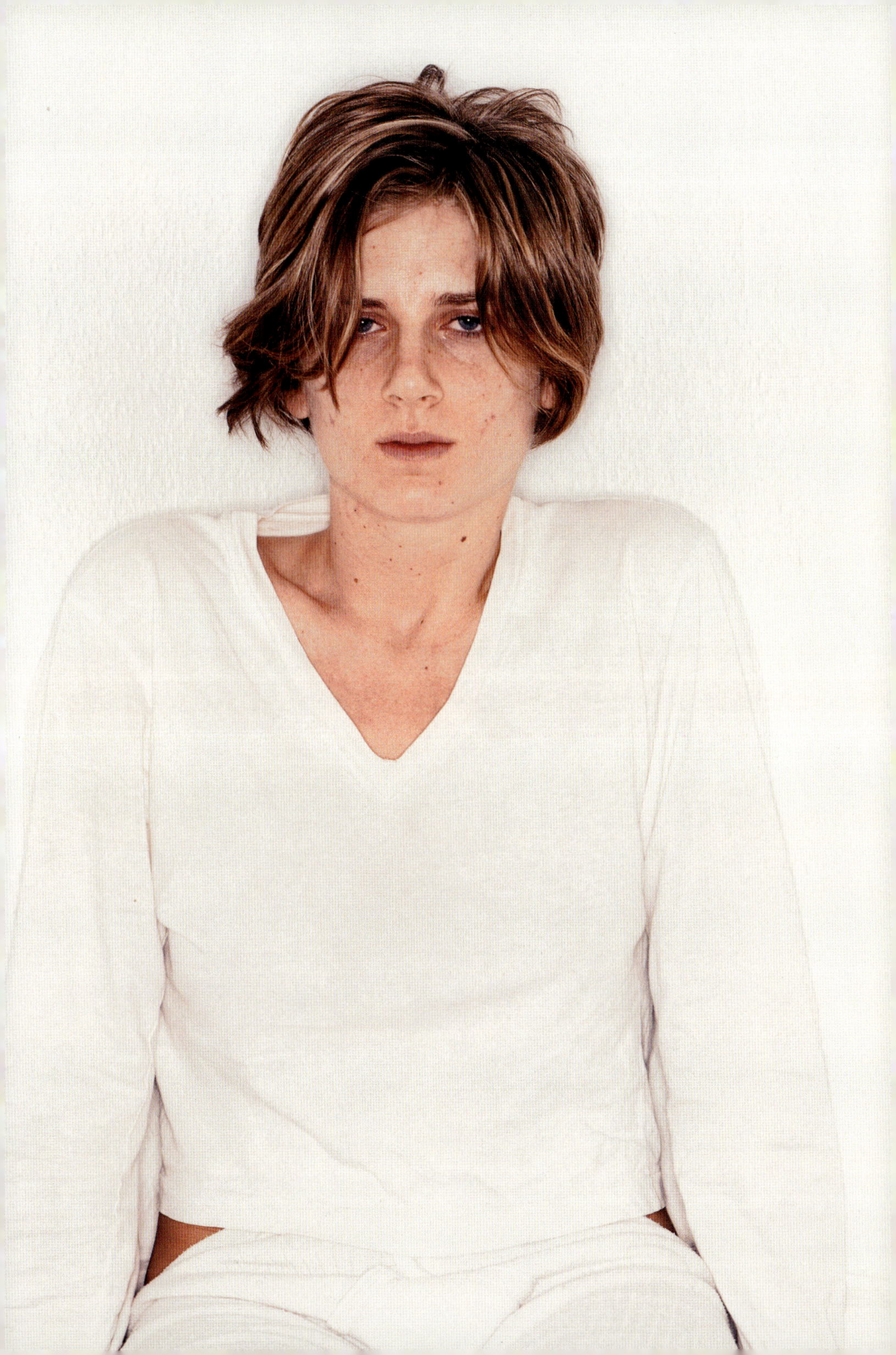

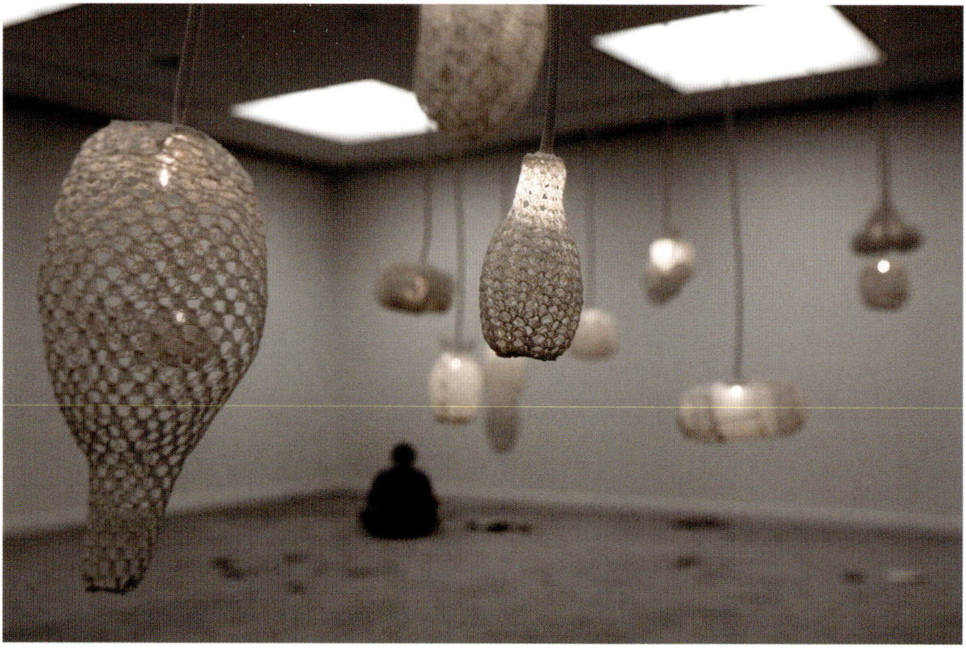

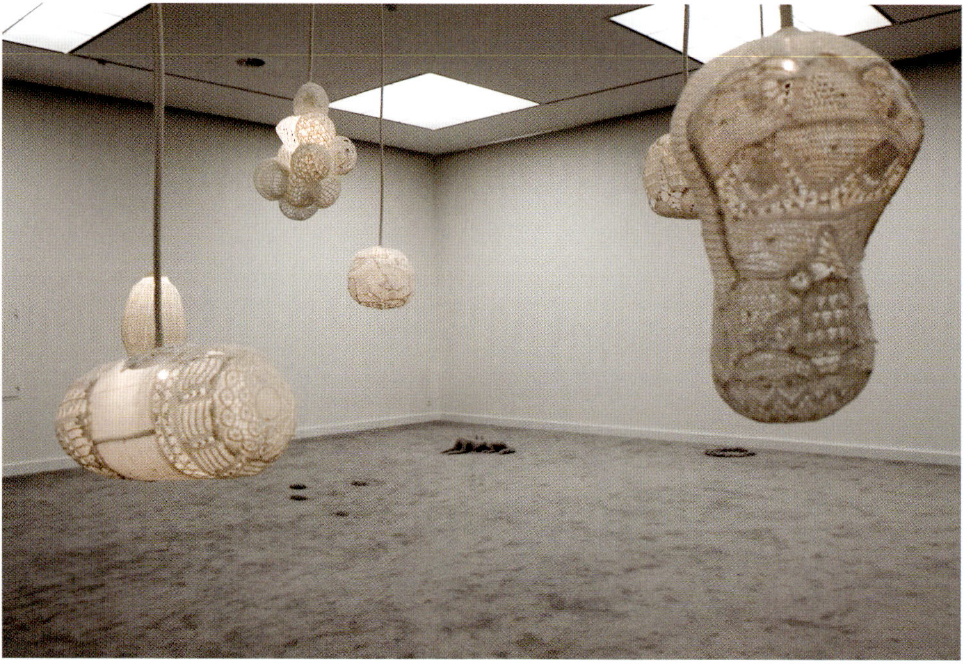

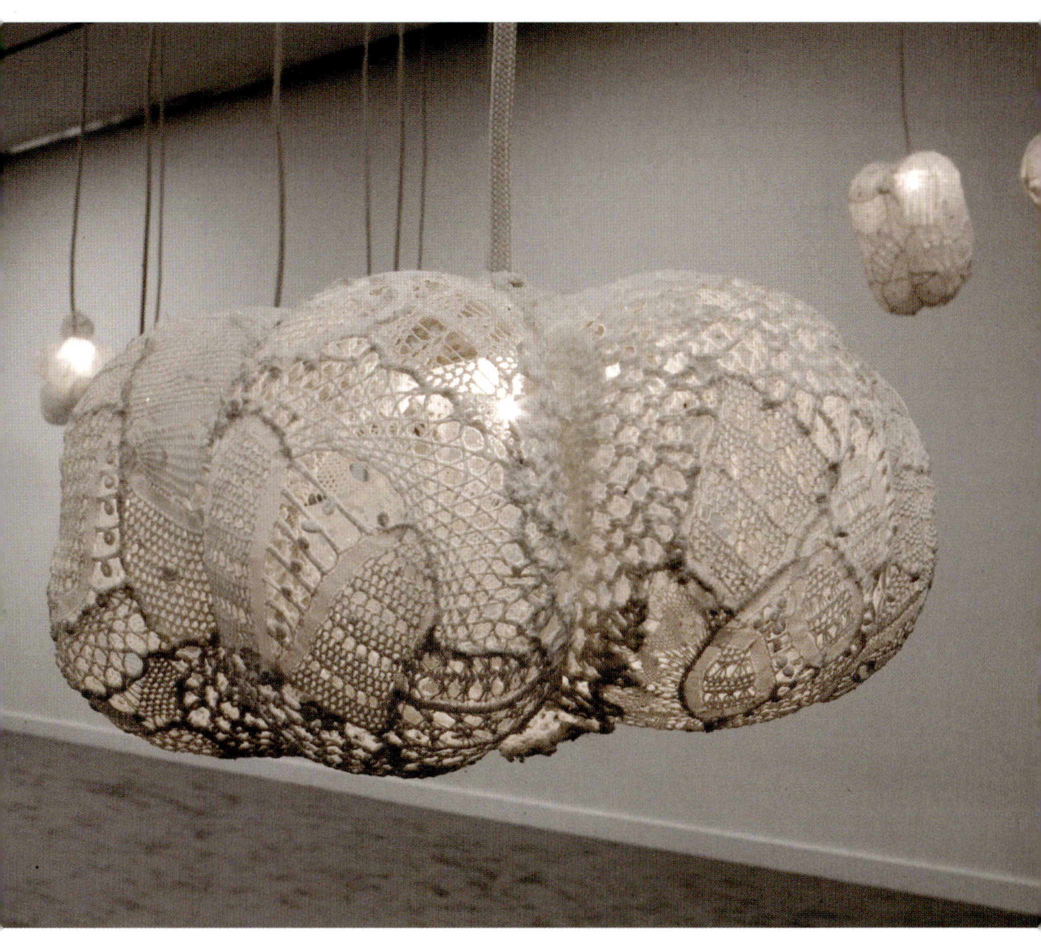

Tonico Lemos Auad
*Sleep Walkers,* 2009
Brazilian and Belgian lace and electric parts, 17 individual hand sewn lanterns. Dimensions variable. Unique in a series of three variations
© the artist. Courtesy the artist and MUHKA (Museum van Hedendaagse Kunst Antwerpen)

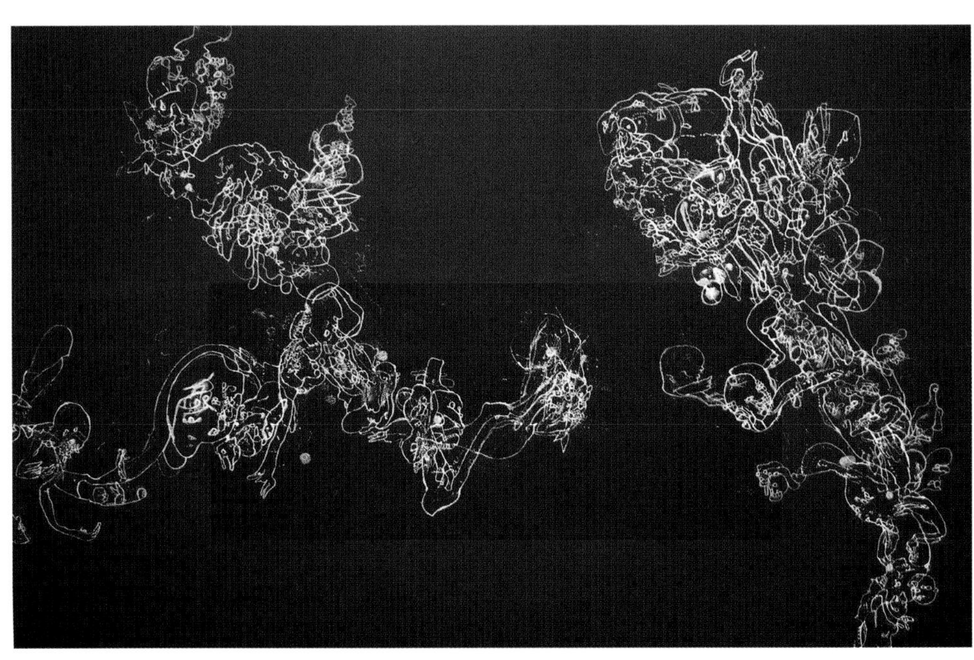

Ed Pien
*Becoming Giant*, 2012
*Soothsayer,* 2012
Ink on sectioned paper,
each 76.2 × 114.3 cm
Courtesy the artist, Pierre-François
Ouellette Art Contemporain,
Montreal, and Birch Libralato, Toronto

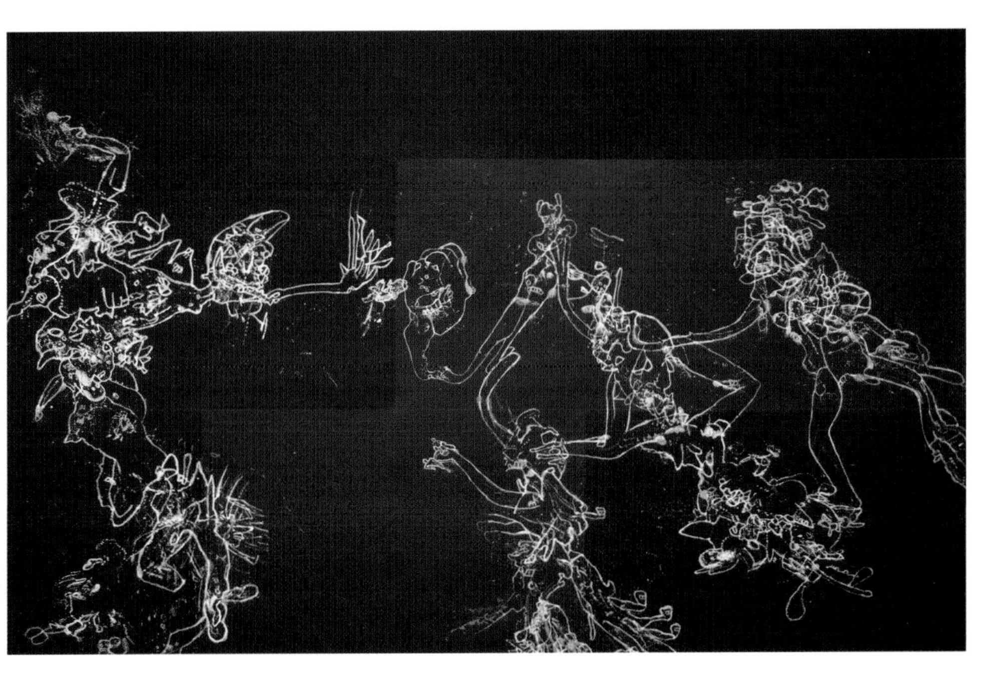

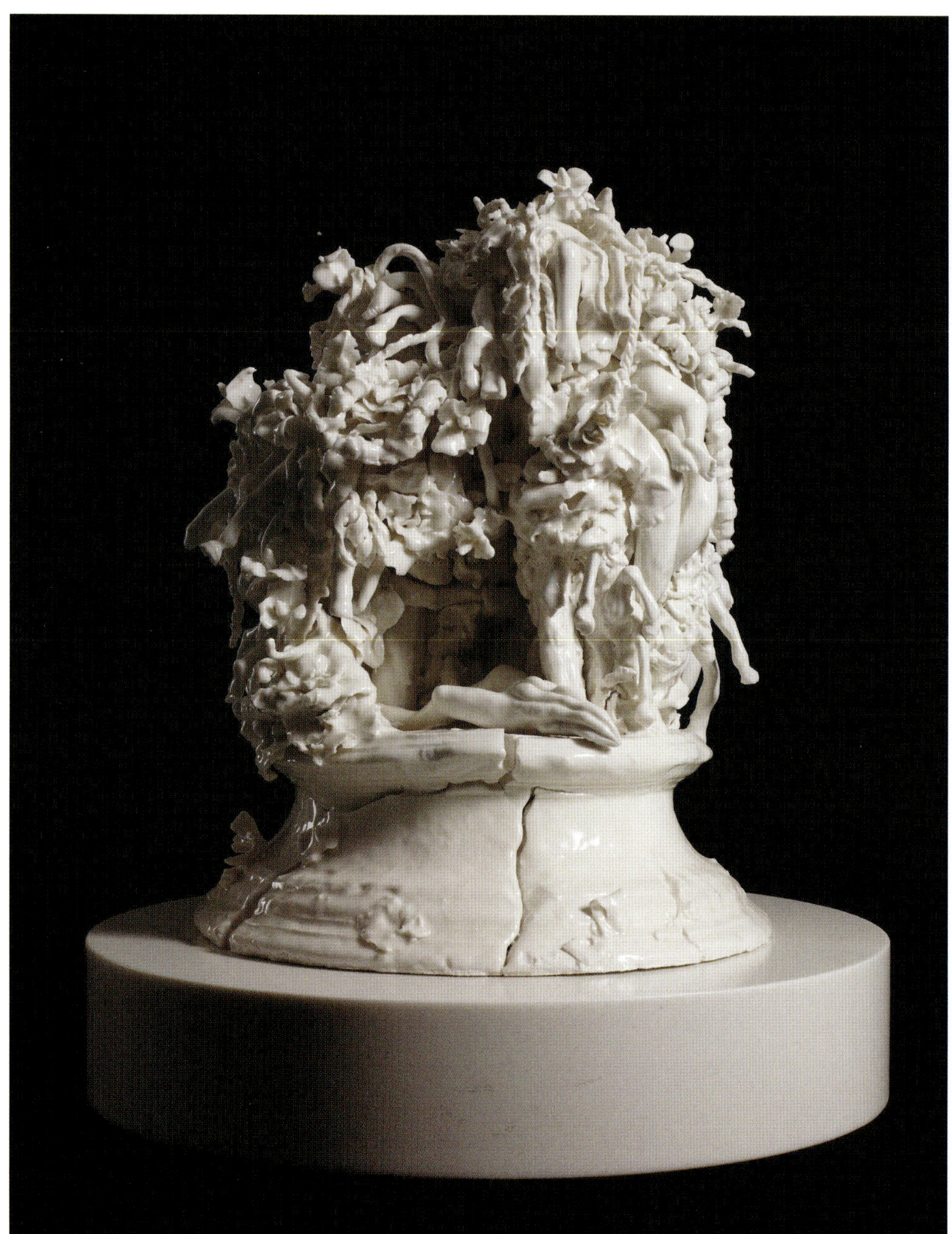

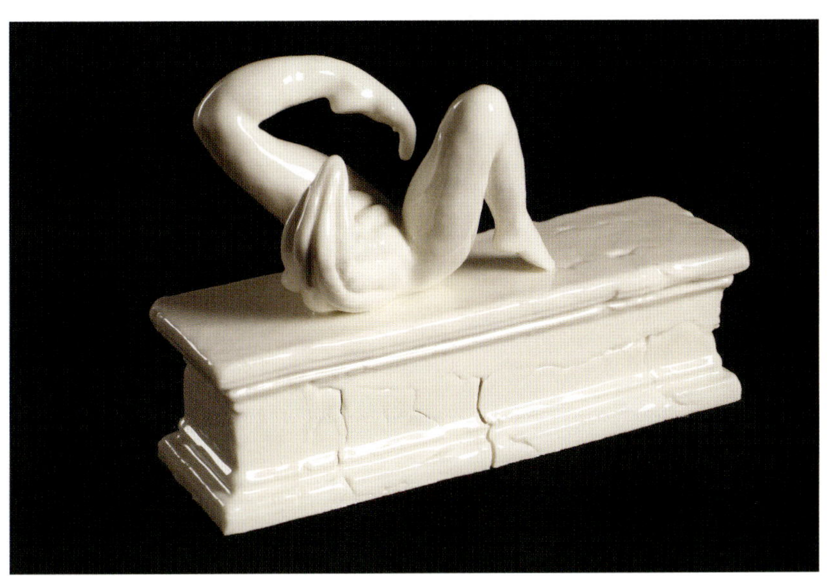

Rachel Kneebone
*At the edge of dawn and darkness*,
2009 (57.2 × Ø 51 cm)
*Study in self sufficiency II*, 2010
(18.2 × 26.2 × 9.6 cm)
*The black shadow projected on
me appeared to elect its prey*, 2012
(69 × Ø 42.5 cm)
All porcelain
Photos: Stephen White (opposite
page and above), Ben Westoby (right)


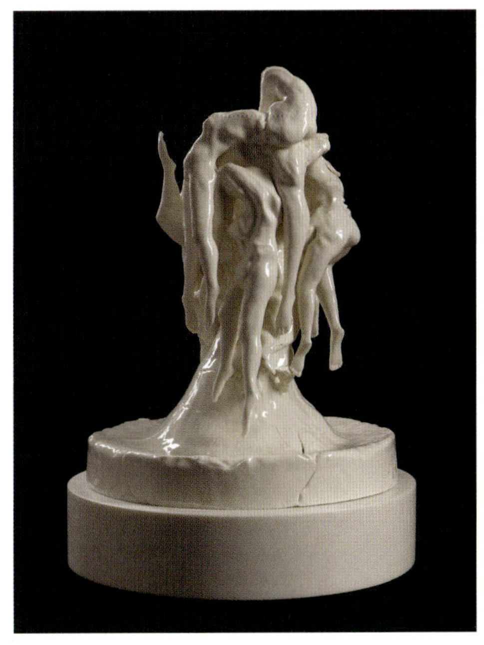

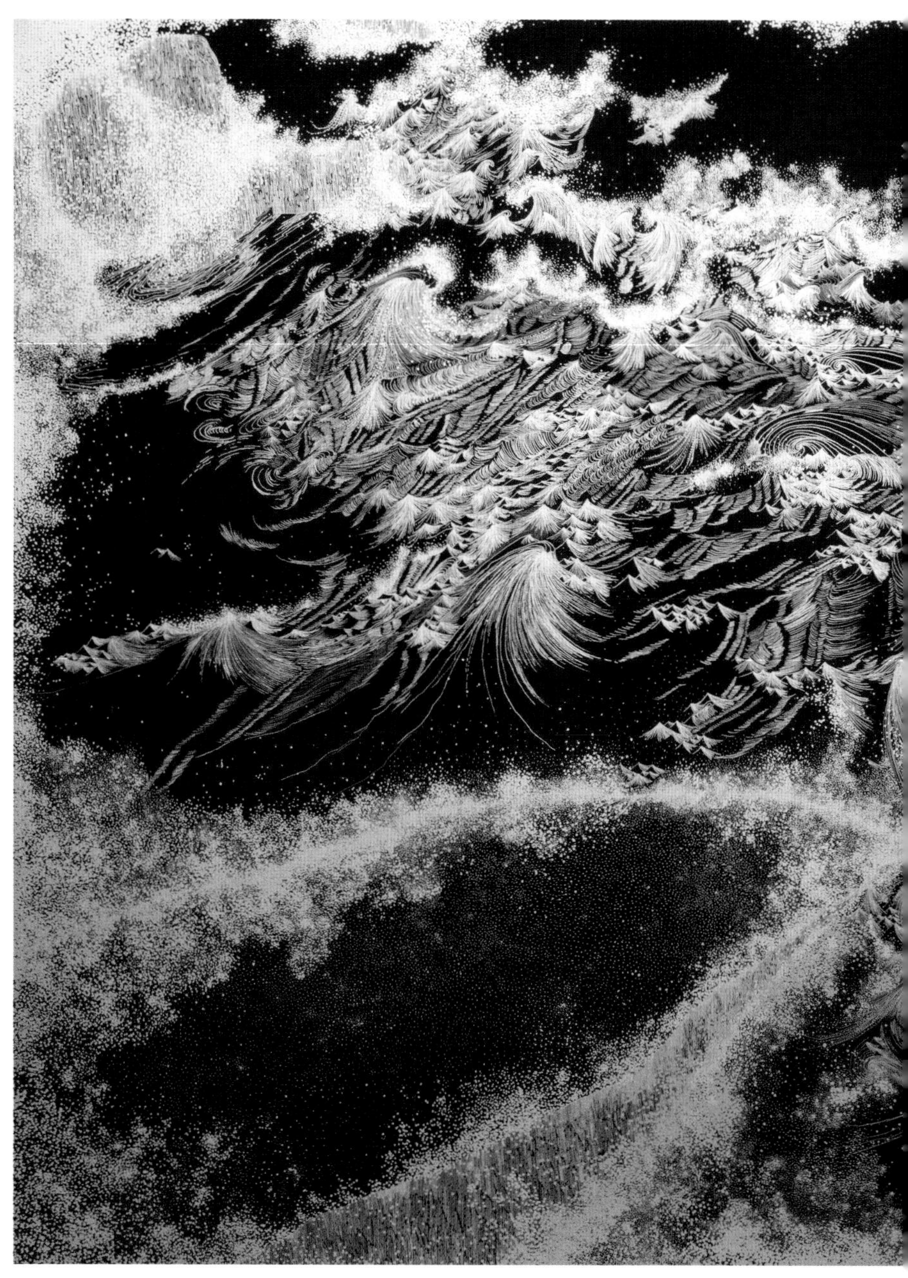

03:00

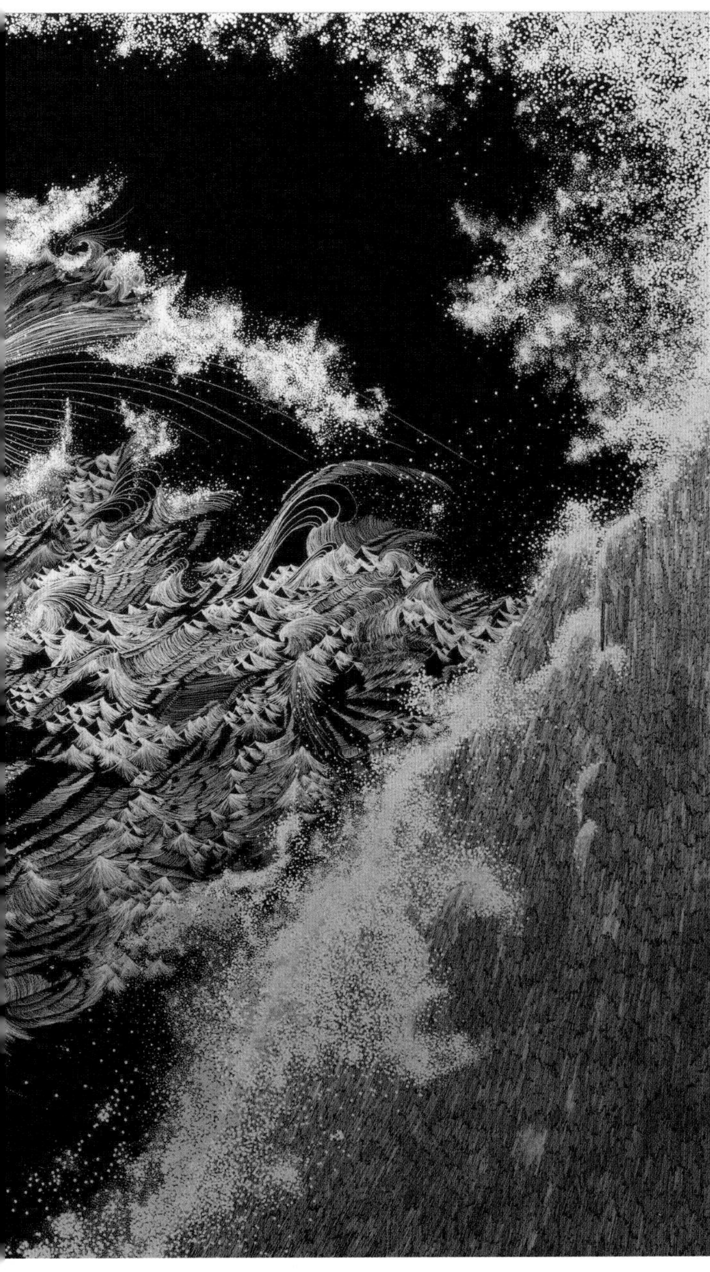

Sandra Cinto
*Untitled,* 2012
Permanent pen and acrylic on canvas, 180 × 250 cm
Private collection
Photo: Ding Musa

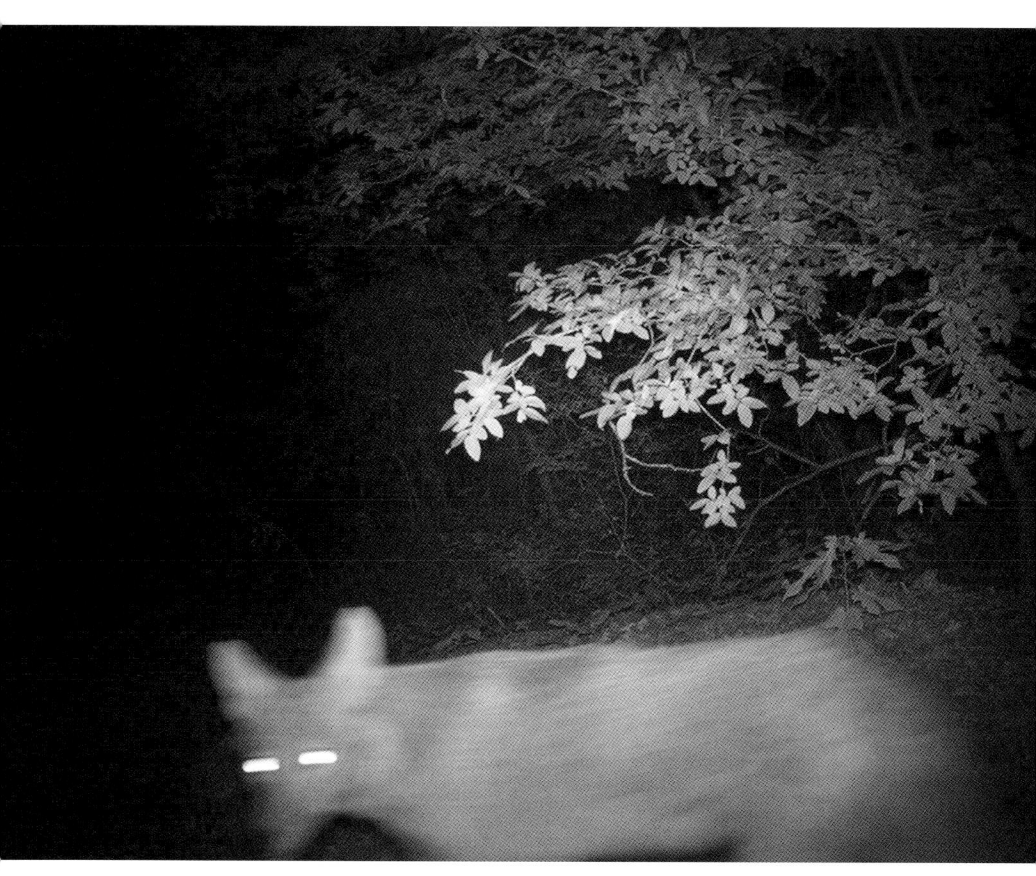

Dornith Doherty
*First Night*, 2011
*Dispute*, 2012
Archival pigment photographs,
each 76.2 × 101.6 cm
Courtesy the artist, Holly Johnson
Gallery and McMurtrey Gallery

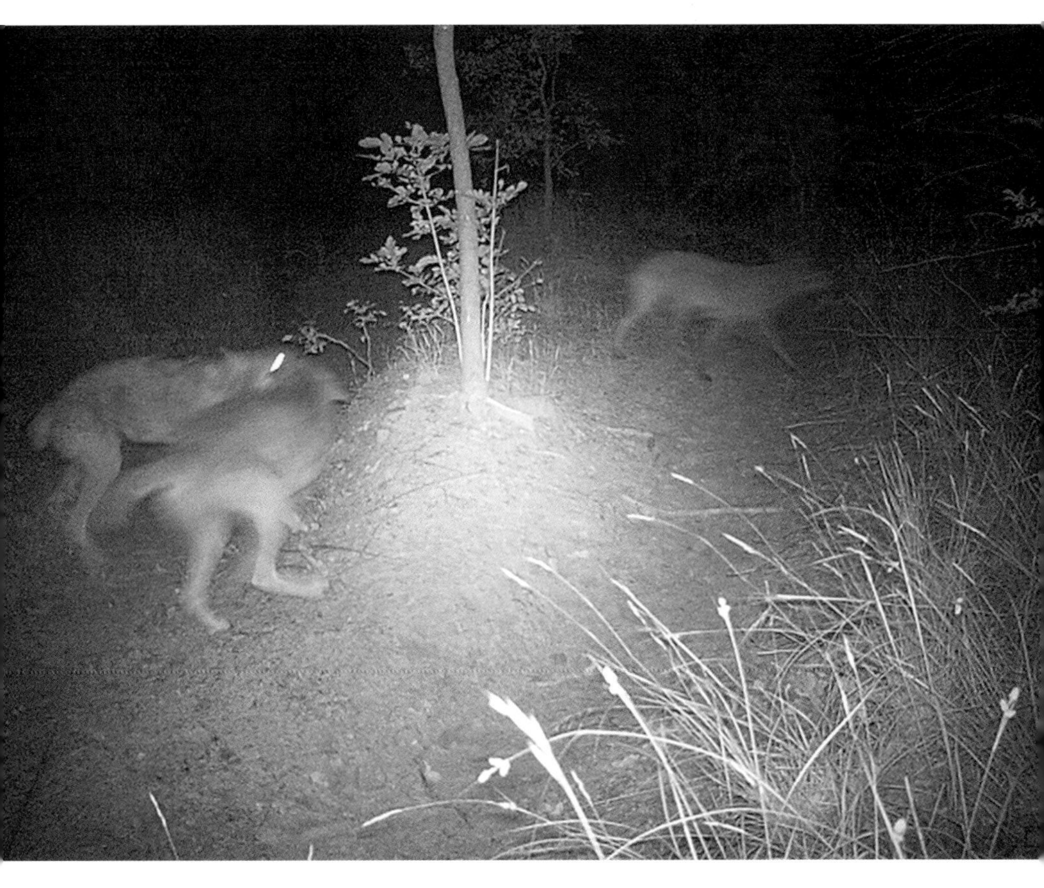

*overleaf*
Lucy Reynolds
*Lake (Nocturne)*, 2009
Still from 16mm film
Courtesy the artist

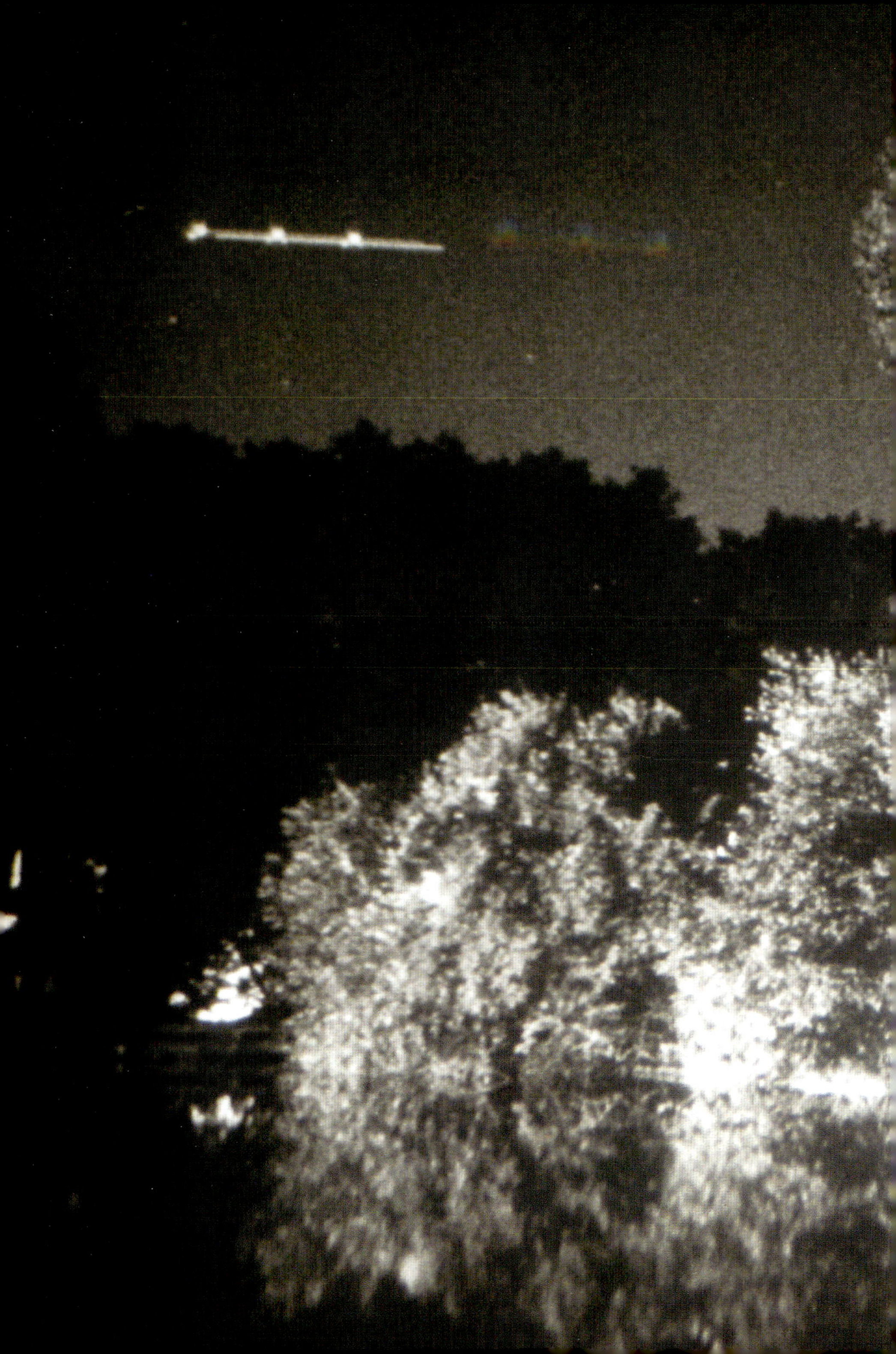

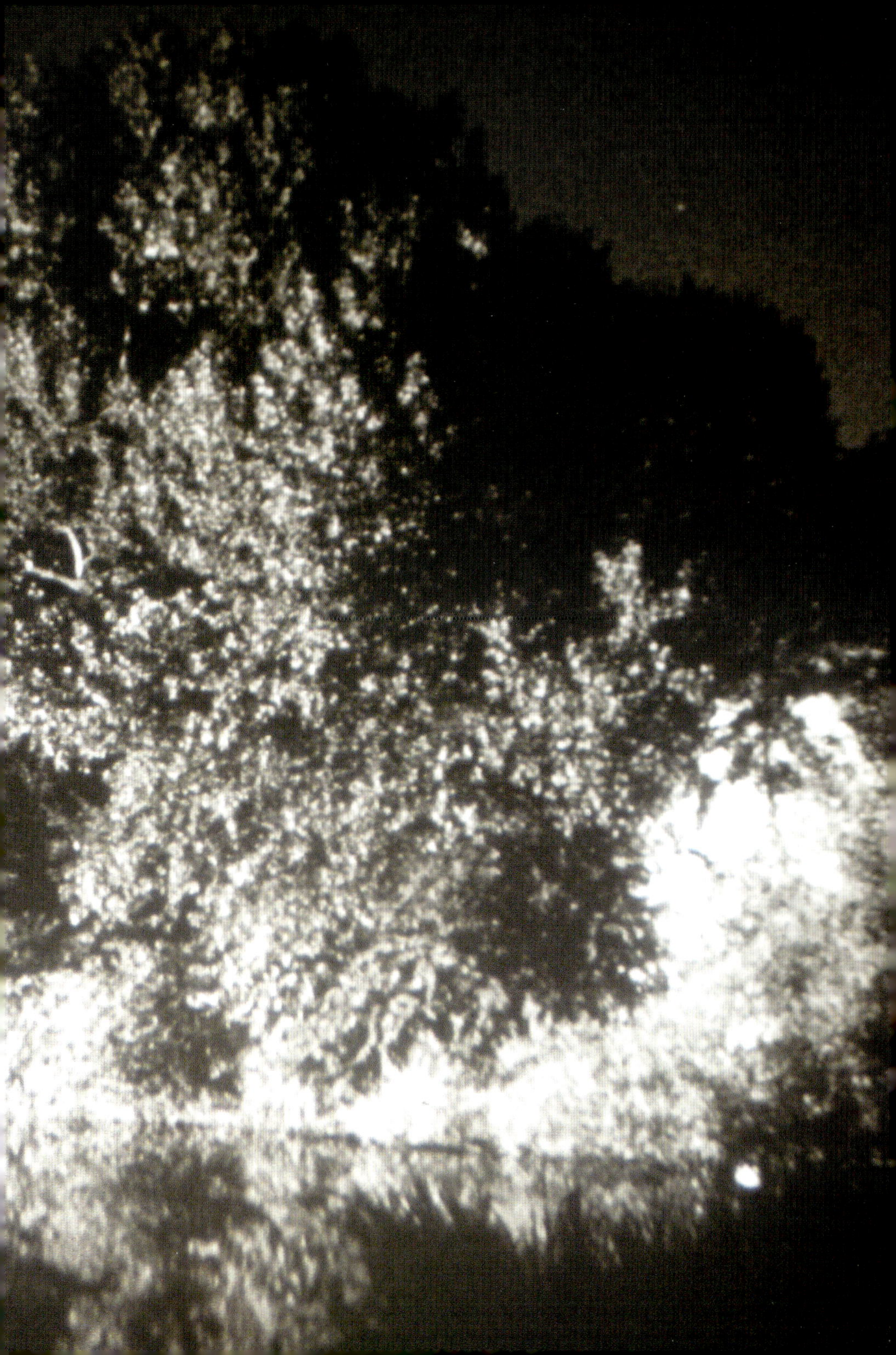

# THE ARTISTS

**Francis Alÿs**
Born 1959, Antwerp. Lives and works in Mexico City.

**Tonico Lemos Auad**
Born 1967, Belem, Brazil. Lives and works in London.

**Jordan Baseman**
Born 1960, Philadelphia. Lives and works in London.

**Sandra Cinto**
Born 1968, Santo André, Brazil. Lives and works in São Paulo.

**Dorothy Cross**
Born 1956, Cork, Ireland. Lives and works in Connemara.

**Dornith Doherty**
Born 1957, Houston, Texas. Lives and works in Southlake, Texas.

**Willi Dorner**
Born 1959, Baden, Austria. Lives and works in Vienna.

**Anthony Goicolea**
Born 1971, Atlanta, Georgia. Lives and works in New York.

**Marc Hulson**
Born 1965, London. Lives and works in London.

**Rachel Kneebone**
Born 1973. Lives and works in London.

**Nathan Mabry**
Born 1978, Durango, Colorado. Lives and works in Los Angeles.

**Michael Palm**
Born 1965, Linz, Austria. Lives and works in Vienna.

**Hirsch Perlman**
Born 1960, Chicago. Lives and works in Los Angeles.

**Ed Pien**
Born 1958, Taipei, Taiwan. Lives and works in Toronto.

**Lucy Reynolds**
Born 1966, London. Lives and works in London.

**Sophy Rickett**
Born 1970, London. Lives and works in London.

**Paul Rooney**
Born 1967, Liverpool. Lives and works in Liverpool.

**Anj Smith**
Born 1978, Kent. Lives and works in London.

**Fred Tomaselli**
Born 1956, Santa Monica, California. Lives and works in Brooklyn, New York.

**Danny Treacy**
Born 1975, Manchester. Lives and works in London.

**Tom Wood**
Born 1951, Ireland. Lived on Merseyside between 1978–2003 before moving to current home in North Wales.

**Bettina von Zwehl**
Born 1971, Munich. Lives and works in London.

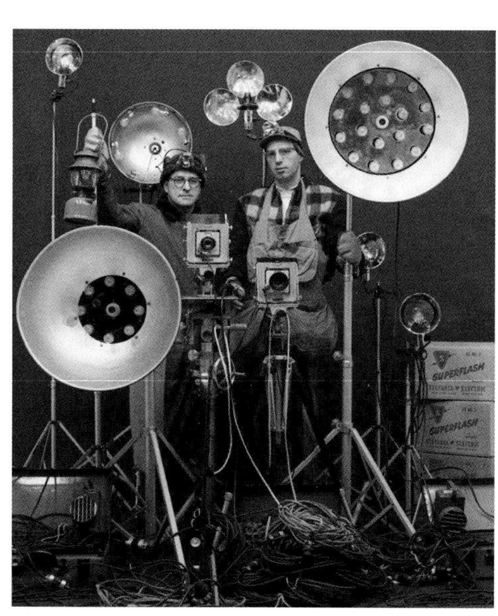


O. Winston Link (1914–2001), *Winston Link, George Thom and night flash equipment (variant),* New York, New York, 1956 (NW795)
Gelatine silver photograph
Signed by O. Winston Link. Courtesy the O. Winston Link Museum, Roanoke, VA. © Conway Link

# EXPOSING THE NIGHT

Sara-Jayne Parsons

As the essence of photography relies on a relationship between light and dark, the camera exists as a perfect conduit for an exploration of the night. As witnessed in several of the works in the exhibition *3 am: wonder, paranoia and the restless night*, there are numerous ways of picturing the small hours. From the use of CCTV and night vision to document the life of animals and the natural world, to late-night/early-morning images of human activities, photography plays a significant role in how the middle of the night is visualised and represented in contemporary art.

Night photographs are often associated with mystery, other-worldliness and fear of the unknown, based on the maxim that the camera sees more than the eye. In the nocturnal reality of a moment like 3 a.m. they reveal secrets through an arc of looking that extends from creative curiosity to surveillance, from the picturesque to the dangerous. It is useful to trace this trajectory by reflecting on a selection of historical precedents to give some context to recent approaches, but also to appreciate further the complicated reality of exposing the night.

Photography is a process that depends on light, a constituent factor that is generally in short supply by natural means at 3 a.m. in most parts of the world. As such, the history of night photography unfolds through a search to overcome darkness; its path is idiosyncratic and experimental, beginning in the 1840s. At this time photographers tried chemical means to capture images at night or in low light by using oxy-hydrogen or 'limelight'. The results were harsh and considered unsatisfactory, particularly from a commercial perspective, as portrait sitters were rendered as pale-faced spectres.

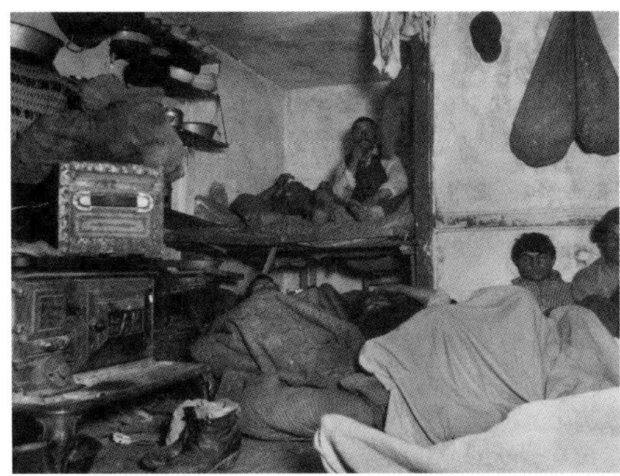

Jacob August Riis (1849–1914)
*Lodgers in Bayard Street Tenement, Five Cents a Spot,* 1889
Gelatine silver print, printed 1957, 15.7 × 12 cm
New York, Museum of Modern Art (MoMA). Gift of the Museum of the City of New York. Acc. n.: 338.1964.


Some of the most imaginative experiments with artificial light were made in the 1860s by Frenchman Gaspard-Félix Tournachon, more popularly known as Nadar. Using electric bunsen batteries and reflectors he photographed in the dark of the sewers and catacombs beneath Paris. The resulting images were ghoulish and macabre, eliciting sensational attention but not really solving the problem of photographing with no or low light. It remained a relatively complicated and expensive business; photographic materials had limited sensitivity and processes required long exposure times. The technology of photography was still in its infancy and it would not be until the mid 1880s that experiments with flash powder resulted in a more successful source of artificial light. Although it was highly explosive and generated dramatic clouds of foul-smelling smoke, the magnesium-based powder proved extremely popular.

One of the first people to experiment with night photography using flash powder was Jacob Riis, an educated, middle-class Danish immigrant working in New York City. As an investigative journalist he recognised photography as a purposeful tool and the camera as an instrument for social change. Along with his reports, he used photographs to provide evidence of the cruel injustices he witnessed in places like Mulberry

Bend, a notorious area of lower Manhattan renowned for its crowded tenements and crime-ridden alleys.

It was Riis' practice to go into lodging houses, quickly set up his view camera and tripod in the dark before disturbing any of the inhabitants, take a photograph and then swiftly retreat as the glare of the flash faded and his dazed subjects began to stir. In many photographs his unsuspecting subjects appear disoriented amidst the clutter and dirt of their surroundings, barely awake, caught by the camera like a startled animal in the middle of the night.

While modern-day critics might question the ethics of Riis' approach, he believed it to be the best way to record disgraceful living conditions. He wanted to shock his late nineteenth-century readers out of their moral complacency and humanise the urban existence of the poor who were largely regarded as a dangerous and unknown entity. He shared his work with social scientists of the time in places like the City Health Department, and he gave public lectures using lantern slides. Riis published his wider findings accompanied by night photographs in *How the Other Half Lives: Studies among the Tenements of New York* (1890).

The 1890s would also see less didactic experiments in night photography by several key practitioners, perhaps most famously Paul Martin in London and Alfred Stieglitz in New York. Both explored a more creative approach to capturing the night, developing a Pictorialist style that considered the aesthetic qualities of photography. They relied on long exposure times and eschewed artificial light, instead seeking out striking juxtapositions of light, shadow and reflection while photographing on dark city streets. Self consciously artistic in their efforts, both often used silhouettes of trees or the effects of bad weather to create a sense of drama and interest in compositions.

For Stieglitz in particular, the subject of the night also provided a creative challenge in the darkroom, and he experimented with printing photogravure on fine art paper, seeking an elegant tonal quality that would complement his soft focus, idealised portraits of the city. In later

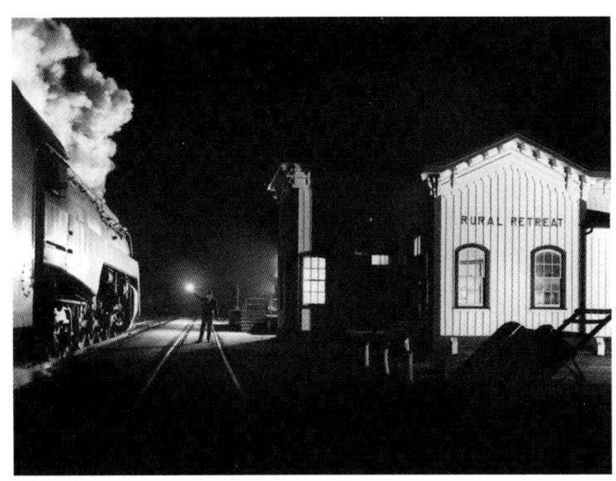


O. Winston Link (1914–2001)
*Highball at Rural Retreat, Virginia,* Rural Retreat, Virginia, 1957 (NW1635)
Gelatine silver photograph
Signed by O. Winston Link (OWLM 2002.8.23).
Courtesy the O. Winston Link Museum, Roanoke, VA.
© Conway Link

years Gyula Halász, better known as Brassaï, perhaps the most famous night photographer of all, continued Stieglitz's nocturnal Pictorialist legacy. His publication *Paris de Nuit* (1932), recognised as the first monograph of night photographs, revealed a hidden, after hours Parisien population of cabaret stars, prostitutes and opium addicts. Compared to Stieglitz who endeavoured to capture empty nocturnal street scenes, Brassaï's lens firmly locates human activity in the night.

By the early 1930s the flash bulb had became widely available, making night photography an easier, less messy proposition. In following decades, photographers exposed the depths of the night as never before, and the results of their surveillance were sometimes shocking. Weegee's candid shots of the streets of New York captured late night crime scenes portraying the aftermath of murder and fire. In such images, fear of the dark night was personified through a narrative of trauma and danger, and 3 a.m. became the perfect time for the paparazzo to prowl.

By contrast, for other photographers the flash bulb meant 3 a.m. was a time to document less sensational activities, which while commonplace, were key in facilitating life in waking hours. This is certainly the case in O. Winston Link's black and white night-time photographs of the Norfolk and Western Railway. Shot along the railroads of the Virginias, North Carolina and Kentucky in the mid 1950s, he captured the last years of one of the great steam-powered train routes of America. Shooting at night because he felt he had better control over lighting the scene, Link devised a complex assembly of coordinated flashes and multiple view cameras that would sometimes take several days to set up.

The resulting photographs are not only a unique document of the power of industry and commerce, but also of small town American life. While focusing on the trains, Link also portrayed rail workers and their communities in close relationship to the railroad, at times resulting in exquisite studies in light and dark. Here the mundane is made heroic, and the night provides a dramatic backdrop for the exposure of human agency generally unseen.

While a penchant for urban and man-made subjects populates the history of night photography to this point, in the latter part of the twentieth century there was a move towards a focus on the natural world. Californian Richard Misrach figures prominently in this paradigm shift. After experimenting with night photography, he began photographing the landscapes of the American West in the mid-1970s.[1] Combining long exposure times with the use of flash, Misrach attempted to capture wilderness on its own terms, as opposed to presenting it as mere scenery

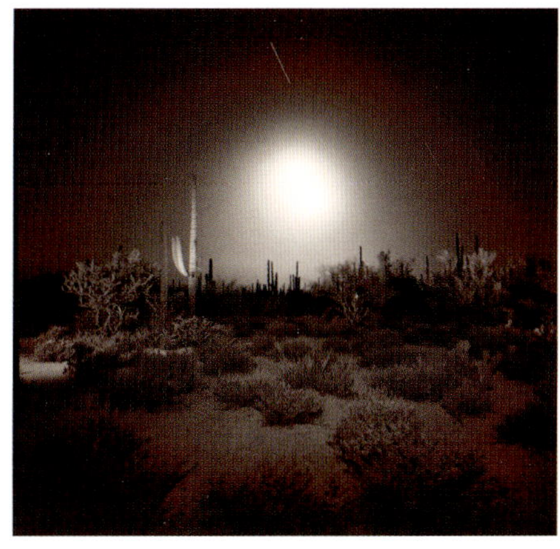

Richard Misrach (b.1949)
*Untitled (Saguaro transition)*, 1977
© Richard Misrach, courtesy Fraenkel Gallery, San Francisco, Marc Selwyn Fine Art, Los Angeles and Pace/MacGill Gallery, New York

to human existence. He continues to photograph the American desert landscape and more recently has fixed on the skies in his viewfinder, capturing the path of constellations and orbiting satellites.

The quiet beauty of Misrach's work suggests a transcendental and metaphorical engagement with the night borne of a contemplation on light and the cosmos. In the history of night photography this is a long way from Nadar's pragmatic underground experiments. And here decades of photographic evolution become apparent. Even though the technology of taking a photograph has changed, the fundamental value of light remains inextricable. Photographers' relationship with light is often extremely intimate; it is something they think about a lot. They look at, measure and consider it in all aspects of their practice, when choosing their subject, waiting for the right time to release the shutter or in the selection of equipment. In the depths of the night this relationship is accentuated and inverted. At 3 a.m. the dark takes over to become the photographer's creative protagonist.

## FURTHER READING


Alland, Alexander. *Jacob A. Riis, Photographer and Citizen*. New York: Aperture, 1974.

*Brassaï*. New York: Museum of Modern Art, 1968.

*Encyclopedia of 20th Century Photography*. New York: Routledge, 2005.

Haworth-Booth, Mark. 'Paul Martin and the Modern Era', in *The Golden Age of British Photography 1839–1900*, London: Aperture, 1984, pp. 184–87.

Hoffman, Katherine. *Stieglitz. A Beginning Light*. New Haven and London: Yale University Press, 2004, pp. 175–77.

Rosenblum, Naomi. *A World History of Photography*. New York: Abbeville Press, 1989.

Stettner, Louis. *Weegee*. New York: Alfred A. Knopft, 1977.


## NOTES

1 In 1974, as a psychology student, Misrach published *Telegraph 3 A.M.: The Street People of Telegraph Avenue, Berkeley, California*, a black and white portrait documentary series of homeless people shot at night. Made into a coffee-table book, he sold the publication to raise money for a food bank, although interestingly, he later questioned the role and legitimacy of the photographer as a political activist in this way.


Sara-Jayne Parsons is Exhibitions Curator at the Bluecoat

# TRAVELS WITH A DONKEY IN THE CÉVENNES

Robert Louis Stevenson

Night is a dead monotonous period under a roof; but in the open world it passes lightly, with its stars and dews and perfumes, and the hours are marked by changes in the face of Nature. What seems a kind of temporal death to people choked between walls and curtains, is only a light and living slumber to the man who sleeps afield. All night long he can hear Nature breathing deeply and freely; even as she takes her rest, she turns and smiles; and there is one stirring hour unknown to those who dwell in houses, when a wakeful influence goes abroad over the sleeping hemisphere, and all the outdoor world are on their feet. It is then that the cock first crows, not this time to announce the dawn, but like a cheerful watchman speeding the course of night. Cattle awake on the meadows; sheep break their fast on dewy hillsides, and change to a new lair among the ferns; and houseless men, who have lain down with the fowls, open their dim eyes and behold the beauty of the night.

At what inaudible summons, at what gentle touch of Nature, are all these sleepers thus recalled in the same hour to life? Do the stars rain down an influence, or do we share some thrill of mother earth below our resting bodies? Even shepherds and old country-folk, who are the deepest read in these arcana, have not a guess as to the means or purpose of this nightly resurrection. Towards two in the morning they declare the thing takes place; and neither know nor inquire further. And at least it is a pleasant incident. We are disturbed in our slumber only, like the luxurious Montaigne, 'that we may the better and more sensibly relish it.' We have a moment to look upon the stars. And there is a special pleasure for some minds in the reflection that we share the impulse with all outdoor creatures in our neighbourhood, that we have escaped out of the Bastille of civilisation, and are become, for the time being, a mere kindly animal and a sheep of Nature's flock.

When that hour came to me among the pines, I wakened thirsty. My tin was standing by me half full of water. I emptied it at a draught; and feeling broad awake after this internal cold aspersion, sat upright to make a cigarette. The stars were clear, coloured, and jewel-like, but not frosty. A faint silvery vapour stood for the Milky Way. All around me the black fir-points stood upright and stock-still. By the whiteness of the pack-saddle, I could see Modestine walking round and round at the length of her tether; I could hear her steadily munching at the sward; but there was not another sound, save the indescribable quiet talk of the runnel over the stones. I lay lazily smoking and studying the colour of the sky, as we call the void of space, from where it showed a reddish grey behind the pines to where it showed a glossy blue-black between the stars. As if to be more like a pedlar, I wear a silver ring. This I could see faintly shining as I raised or lowered the cigarette; and at each whiff the inside of my hand was illuminated, and became for a second the highest light in the landscape.

A faint wind, more like a moving coolness than a stream of air, passed down the glade from time to time; so that even in my great chamber the air was being renewed all night long. I thought with horror of the inn at Chasseradès and the congregated nightcaps; with horror of the nocturnal prowesses of clerks and students, of hot theatres and pass-keys and close rooms. I have not often enjoyed a more serene possession of myself, nor felt more independent of material aids. The outer world, from which we cower into our houses, seemed after all a gentle habitable place; and night after night a man's bed, it seemed, was laid and waiting for him in the fields, where God keeps an open house. I thought I had rediscovered one of those truths which are revealed to savages and hid from political economists: at the least, I had discovered a new pleasure for myself. And yet even while I was exulting in my solitude I became aware of a strange lack. I wished a companion to lie near me in the starlight, silent and not moving, but ever within touch. For there is a fellowship more quiet even than solitude, and which, rightly understood, is solitude made perfect. And to live out of doors with the woman a man loves is of all lives the most complete and free.

As I thus lay, between content and longing, a faint noise stole towards me through the pines. I thought, at first, it was the crowing of cocks or the barking of dogs at some very distant farm; but steadily and gradually it took articulate shape in my ears, until I became aware that a passenger was going by upon the high-road in the valley, and singing loudly as he went. There was more of good-will than grace in his performance; but he trolled with ample lungs; and the sound of his voice took hold upon the hillside and set the air shaking in the leafy glens. I have heard people passing by night in sleeping cities; some of them sang; one, I remember, played loudly on the bagpipes. I have heard the rattle of a cart or carriage spring up suddenly after hours of stillness, and pass, for some minutes, within the range of my hearing as I lay abed. There is a romance about all who are abroad in the black hours, and with something of a thrill we try to guess their business. But here the romance was double: first, this glad passenger, lit internally with wine, who sent up his voice in music through the night; and then I, on the other hand, buckled into my sack, and smoking alone in the pine-woods between four and five thousand feet towards the stars.

Extract from *Travels with a Donkey in the Cévennes* by Robert Louis Stevenson (1912), Chatto & Windus, London. Reproduced by kind permission of Random House Group Limited.

# THE POWERS OF INSOMNIA

Elisabeth Bronfen

While insomniacs want to be engulfed by sleep, they find themselves absorbed instead by a different nocturnal state. They live the state of being neither fully awake (which is to say distracted from any encounter with oneself by the imagined presence of others) nor protected from oneself by the oblivion sleep affords. Indeed, what most insomniacs agree upon, regardless of how they eventually come to evaluate this experience, is that sleeplessness inflicts upon them a radical sense of solitude, a heightened sense of being separate from others, alone with one's thoughts, one's affects, with the sensations of one's body. Neither sharing the night with others nor shielded from it by virtue of sleep, they feel themselves to be abandoned and unprotected in an encounter with the violent onslaught of their unresolved emotions.

Yet the manner in which insomniacs describe what they experience during their sleepless nights is highly diverse. While the common denominator is an acute sense of isolation, of inhabiting a world apart from all other human beings, some may experience this as a delirious sense of nothingness, as a painful experience of deprivation. For others, however, such a radical confrontation with their own solitude can result in a state of megalomania, a heightened sense of being privileged because privy to an insight denied those who spend the night sleeping. Because insomniacs are too close to sleep to be able to distract themselves by reading, and thus entering into someone else's fictional reality, they find themselves cruelly tied to their own fantasy world, unable to escape from themselves. Fearing the emotions, evocations, and memories about to emerge, insomniacs believe they have nothing to fear in sleep, and yet something must be more attractive, perhaps even necessary in the state of heightened sensual awareness, which results instead in a resistance to sleep. It is as though the hyper-awareness of the sounds around them, of the vast empty space enclosing them, of the pulsations of their own bodies, were an answer to an unacknowledged fear – namely that succumbing to sleep could be considered tantamount to entering a state of deathlike oblivion. Indeed, the question insomniacs find themselves returning to incessantly is why it is more attractive for them to endure the journey through a sleepless night, vacillating between a desire for sleep and an acceptance of their dreadful solitude, rather than to cede themselves utterly to their unconscious. Or put another way, what is more terrifying about sleep, supposedly the time of peaceful restitution, that compels the insomniac to resist it at all costs? Is insomnia as much a mode of protection against being engulfed by sleep as it prohibits the protection sleep is meant to afford?

---

What is rendered acutely visible, when one compares descriptions that insomniacs offer of this sleeping disorder, is that while some complain about the suffering they experience during their nocturnal solitude, others celebrate the absence of sleep as an experience of infinite richness. Precisely because sleeplessness forces one to return to oneself, indeed prohibits all distraction from a radical encounter with oneself, it proves, for some at least, to be the source of creativity; it makes unacknowledged or forbidden knowledge accessible, such that one is able to experience things one would be incapable of during the day. Apodictically put: crossing sleep with wakefulness, crossing rational consciousness with a lucidity that comes from abandoning the state of mind one harbors during day, the insomniac can experience a magnificent sense of concentration because he or she is liberated from all distractions, from all pressures to perform, to interact with others. Insomniacs seem to enter a state of pure existing in the present, experiencing themselves and the world they inhabit, without taking note, without processing it, without performing in it.

Extracts from *The Powers of Insomnia* by Elisabeth Bronfen. Publication: Louise Bourgeois *The Insomnia Drawings*, edited and published by Daros, Zurich (2000). 

# HOPE FADES FOR THE HOSTAGES

Ailsa Cox

Every night and every morning. Two red zeros staring straight back at you. Exactly three a.m. A surprise. Not a surprise. The scent of a sleeping body lying by your side in the darkness. The steady puff and blow of breathing. Gentle, slowly now, do not disturb. The dead grate in the living room. The carpet threaded by silver trails. The house feels abandoned and hollow, and you yourself are its wandering ghost, pouring a whiskey, reading last week's papers while you're waiting for tomorrow. *Hope fades for the hostages.* Won't be up long. But this time it's different. A noise. Not just the wind sawing the trees, or the hum of the fridge, or a car swishing by. Something else, a dripping sound. Something dripping. Hold your breath and listen. You almost think it's stopped. But there it is again, a little louder, gentle, insistent. Upstairs the sleeper dreams on, unaware.

*It's three in the morning. I'm writing this letter thirty thousand feet above the surface of the planet, the cabin lights down and the passengers snoozing, their bodies strapped in, slumped under the blankets, their faces gone slack and their mouths hanging open. You know I can't sleep with this weird congregation of strangers, hate making these trips to the ends of the earth. When it's three in the morning, back home in England, it'll be 3 p.m. in Eastern Siberia. Dream of me while I'm talking landfalls and terminals with Mr Kim in the Chukotka Suite at the Hotel Anadyr.*

They pull in at the motorway services, a constellation of low roofs floating somewhere in the void between departure and arrival. Frank has stopped here before, or his shadow has lingered, waiting for change from the fat man at the till. 'Can I interest you … ?' pointing at the giant Aeros, mint and orange flavour, hurrying back to the van, coffee spilling on his sleeve, the muddy verges sucking at his shoes. He didn't want to stop, if it wasn't for the rain he would have kept on driving, but he can't see the road for the mist and the spray of the lorries. Beneath the duvet, Linda's breathing seems to be slower and hoarser, but she's okay, she's just sleeping. 'We're fine,' he says out loud, 'we'll make it.' She knows that he would never let her down.

A tiny drop of water in the corner of the bay, how could you have not ever seen that before, and the cracks, new cracks everywhere, and the old ones spreading inexorably, and what have you done about it, nothing, not a thing, to stop that inevitable progress, until the whole place splits apart like the House of Usher. Bed down on the sofa. There will be no more sleeping. Your brain's reeled in and yanked to the surface, and the small plangent sound of the drip punctuates the long hours like an irregular pulse, and it's all the fault of the sleeper upstairs who said the house was solid, and he could do the work himself, and the only bucket you can find to catch the leak has got a hole in the bottom, why would you keep a bucket with a hole, and why are there so many chairs in this house … ?

*On the world map, England's tiny, the British Isles just an outcrop, crumbled from the jagged edge of Europe. Flip the page round, and what do you get? On either side, the great mass of North America and Russia, and in between them a white patch, the Arctic, a white patch which is shrinking, and it is because the ice is melting that Mr Kim plans to send ships through to sink a cable which will cut the London-Tokyo latency by sixty milliseconds. Not much to you and me, but if you're an algorithmic trader you get very excited by this kind of thing. Imagine a great snake nipping the toe of Cornwall, dipping down to the ocean floor, plunging across the Atlantic, hundreds of feet below the surface, amongst those deep sea creatures barely glimpsed by human eye, heading through the North West Passage and on to Murmansk, looping over the roof of Russia en route for Japan.*

She's so frail, there's nothing to her, when he lifts her she might float away, but she begged him, begged him, to drive her to Truro. Another week or two, and they could have brought the baby to see her, but the worse she became the harder it was to say an outright no. So an if became a maybe and then a probability, and before he could stop himself he was bedding her down on a mattress in the back of the camper van, which was not something you really should be doing, but the van was running like clockwork, and there was no reason they should be pulled over, and she was no less comfortable there than she'd be anywhere else. More comfortable in some ways – it reminded her of when they used to go all over the place, parked up by rivers and roadsides. If they set off in the evening when the roads were so much quieter, they could be at their daughter's in five or six hours. That was before the weather came down. But not to worry, they can still make it. He sends a quick text to his daughter, telling her not to wait up, and she sends something long and angry back to him within seconds. Can't do right for doing wrong. Isn't that always the case? When he starts the ignition, it makes a rasping sound, and they've hardly left the services behind before he's on the hard shoulder, rain trickling down his neck, desperately trying to bring the engine back to life.

… and what does he do all day, what does he do, he goes round junk shops buying chairs that need fixing and comparing the prices they might fetch on eBay, and if you call someone in to give you an estimate for the plastering it'll be a slur on his manhood, and besides those are cracks that can't be skimmed over, fissures and canyons running deep inside the brickwork, and even as you lie there the drip is getting louder and he just won't care, say it's *par for the course*, an old house, decrepit, same as you and me, and he'll make a show of senility, sounding a bass note on the solar plexus, and screwing his face into a caricature, winding you up, like when he talks about growing his hair and it looks awful. He spends money buying you beautiful things, an emerald necklace or an old lithograph, but you don't want anything, you don't want any *things*, and it comes to you that what you want for your birthday – what you'd really like – is for him to just get a hair cut.

*Of course this is all on paper. It might not ever happen. If you check the Bude and Stratton Post, the news is still the falling quality of the local bathing water and the impact of bad weather on the tourist season – not a word about any trans-Arctic project starting on the beach. And yet somewhere on the globe they're talking billions of dollars. Deals are being brokered, torn up and rewritten between cartels and oligarchs, speculators and major providers – every spin of the wheel setting smaller cogs in motion, sending PR men and security consultants and engineers like me, boarding planes in the hope of securing a contract, keeping an eye on those other passengers in blue shirts staring shifty-eyed at their smart phones shortly after the safety lights switch off. My job is simple. I do the drawings. Whether it happens or not, that doesn't matter to me.*

What a fucking moron. Putting petrol in the tank instead of diesel – he's seen plenty of other fucking idiots do it – what else could it be – and what in Christ's name has he done, bringing her straight to the hour of her death? That's what he keeps thinking, as he works in the driving rain by torchlight, keeps thinking and remembering something that's stuck in his mind – three o'clock, they say that's the turning point, if he doesn't get her safe by three she won't survive. There's no help, never was, not the carrot juice or the vitamin pills or the positive thinking, just the hope of a miracle, the faint possibility that he's wrong and it's no more than a faulty connection. The phone buzzes in his pocket, but he can't bear to answer because that'll be Dawn again, and she won't leave it to him, she'll want to call an ambulance, and that's something Frank can't do. He cannot send Linda to hospital.

So now you've decided. Everything's clear. Tomorrow you'll have that conversation which will mark the first step towards a new beginning. Not even the drip seems so bad after all. Not even the cracks in the wall. You're ready to creep back up to bed, and curl up besides the sleeper, rehearsing what you're going to say when morning comes. Squeezing past a set of dining chairs stashed in the hallway, you set foot on the stairs, listening for the steady puff of his breathing, and suddenly it seems that you're stepping on a gangplank and the house is swaying with the motion of the sea. He's standing there waiting to help you aboard, but what kind of ship this is, and where you're sailing, is something that is yet to be explained.

*The only thing that keeps me sane, cooped up in this vacuum, is the thought of sealing the envelope, and somehow finding a stamp and a postbox in a wasteland of snow and barbed wire. Of course it won't really be like that. The town will be pretty much the same as any other – a grid of office blocks between the mountains and the harbour, the last trace of snow just a passing reminder. In the Chukotka Suite, I'll pause to take off my watch for rewinding, just as I always do at the start of presentations. 'Yes,' I'll say, if there's any reaction, 'it's hand made, an anniversary present, as a matter of fact. My wife knows I like old-fashioned things.' Ah, wives – a small murmur of laughter. By then this letter will be on its way. One day I'll come back from work to read your name on the envelope, and I'll keep it with all the others in case you decide to come home.*

But in the end there's no alternative. That's what he tells Linda. The van's fucked. So some one's going to have to come and get them. Just too bad. But at least they're nearly there, and she can see the baby tomorrow. A few more miles, that's all. He hates the sound of his own cheery voice. Everything he's saying sounds like a lie, even the things that are true. But she seems no worse. She's even taking a mouthful of soup from the flask. 'Do you remember,' she keeps saying. 'Do you remember when we …?' He can't make out what she's saying and there's no time to ask before he hears the sound of the ambulance screeching like an owl.

Ailsa Cox is a short story writer based at Edge Hill University, Ormskirk, Lancashire. Her collection, *The Real Louise*, is published by Headland Press.

# WHY DO WE SLEEP?

Leon Kreitzman

A rat prevented from sleeping will lose the ability to maintain body heat and die of no apparent cause in about three weeks. As most parents of young children know, sleep deprivation is a form of torture that rapidly saps the ability to think and perform cognitive tasks. There is a rare human condition in which the sufferer loses the ability to sleep and dies in a matter of months.

It seems that humans need to sleep but the question is why? Also, we seem to require a certain amount of sleep to function optimally. A third question is whether we need to get our daily sleep ration all in one go or whether we can take it as a series of naps?

After all, cutting down on sleep would be the easiest way to solve the time shortage. There is some evidence that this has been happening. One study has suggested that contemporary American students sleep two hours less a night than their counterparts at the turn of the century.[1] But too little sleep causes its own problems.

Nobody has any very good reason as to why we need to sleep. Our hunter-gatherer ancestors in the African savannah probably had to be active during the day because they had to see what they were doing.[2] Gathering berries, nuts and roots by day when it was light was much easier as humans have relatively poor nocturnal vision – or at least modern humans have. If early humans had a poor sense of smell and inadequate nocturnal vision then returning to the family cave with a bunch of poisonous berries was not a recipe for evolutionary survival. Likewise, hunting was a daytime pursuit for humans who were more likely to be the hunted at night.

That does not explain why we sleep, only why our early ancestors may have stayed in at night. They could have conserved energy by resting without the need to actually lose consciousness and fall asleep. Daniel Dennett, director of a Centre for Cognitive Studies, solves the problem to his own satisfaction when he suggests that sleep does not need a 'clear, biological function'.[3] He turns the question upside down and suggests that it is being awake that demands explanation. According to Dennett, 'a life of sleep is as good a life as any and in many regards better, certainly cheaper, than most.' Dennett deliberately overstates his point, and for humans sleep would seem to be maladaptive. One of the distinguishing characteristics of human beings and the key to their evolutionary success is the capacity to learn. Although generations of children have believed that learning can occur osmotically by putting the answers under their pillow the night before an examination, there is no good evidence that this is how it happens. Being awake imparts a cost in terms of energy usage but it does have a certain educational value.

Sleep is presumed to benefit the brain perhaps by giving neurones a chance to recuperate. The frenetic neuronal activity during rapid eye movement (REM) sleep that punctuates our nights suggest we doze to consolidate memories. Francis Crick, co-discoverer with James Watson of the double helix structure of DNA, put forward the idea that when we dream, mental junk is being eliminated. According to Crick we sleep to forget. However, it has been suggested that the rapid eye movements are merely a way of stirring the vitreous humour in the eye, so ensuring that a reasonable supply of oxygen reaches the cornea during sleep.

Recent work suggests that sleep is linked to the immune system. Sleep deprived rats have high numbers of bacterial pathogens that are normally suppressed by the immune system.[4] In humans, even moderate sleep deprivation has a detectable influence on immune system cells. The immune system seems to affect sleep in return. Infections are well known to cause sleepiness and it has been shown that several cytokines, molecules that regulate immune response, can by themselves induce slumber. Cytokines have a direct effect on neural development and in rats, at least, it has been demonstrated that a gene for one cytokine becomes more active in the brain during sleep.[5] It is known that no damage to the brain prevents sleep indefinitely, so sleep must involve a benefit to neural functioning. While it is still speculation, the idea has been put forward that cytokine activity during sleep reconditions the synapses, the junctions between the neurons, thereby solidifying memories.[6] Linking sleep with the immune system offers a plausible evolutionary pathway for sleep in humans. A positive feedback loop may be involved between cytokine production, sleep and memory which could result in survival advantages. Improvements in memory and consequently in learning capacity and what we would call experience would be of benefit to early humans.

Whatever the reasons, missing even one night's sleep causes problems. In the USA 47 per cent of workers experienced at least one episode of sleeplessness in the previous three months.[7] Two-thirds of those who had trouble sleeping say they had a harder time getting through the day as a result.

The familiar culprits of stress, anxiety and worry contribute to most long nights spent staring at the ceiling: 48 per cent of sleepless workers blame stress and anxiety. But aches and pains may also be a factor. Although they do not report pain as the main reason for sleeplessness, 42 per cent of workers say their inability to sleep was accompanied by physical discomfort.

Workers who have trouble sleeping experience it on a fairly regular basis, an average of eight times per month. And there are indications that the trouble is more severe when the workday is near. On a typical work night, 49 per cent of people with sleep problems sleep six or fewer hours. On weekends, the share drops to 30 per cent.

A rough night can wreak havoc at work the next day: 63 per cent of workers who have trouble sleeping find it harder to handle stress on the job, and 60 per cent say they have difficulty concentrating. More than half find it hard to listen or solve problems. When asked to quantify these problems, people say that after a sleepless night their concentration is only 70 per cent of normal, they accomplish about 76 per cent of what they usually can do, and the quality of their work reaches only 80 per cent of normal. This opinion of the bad effects of sleeplessness carries over to others who do not get enough rest. More than eight in ten people believe that their co-workers' problem-solving, concentration and ability to handle stress decline when they do not get enough sleep.[8]

## NOTES

1 Michael Young, *The Metronomic Society*, Thames & Hudson 1988.
2 Stanley Coren, *The Sleep Thieves*, The Free Press 1996.
3 Daniel Dennett, *Darwin's Dangerous Idea*, Penguin 1995.
4 Carol Everson (University of Tennessee), *Scientific American*, July 1996.
5 James Kreuger (University of Tennessee), *Scientific American*, July 1996.
6 *ibid*.
7 National Sleep Foundation, *Sleeplessness, Pain and the Workplace,* National Sleep Foundation 1995.
8 *ibid*.

# THE WILD PLACES

Robert Macfarlane

Up on the ridge, the blizzard blew for two hours. I lay low, got cold, watched the red reeds that poked up from the ice flicker in the wind. Hail fell in different shapes, first like pills, then in a long shower of rugged spheres the size of peppercorns. Over half an hour, the hail turned to snow, which had the texture of salt and fell hissing on to the ice. I had begun to feel cold, deep down, as though ice were forming inside me, floes of it cruising my core, pressure ridges riding up through my arms and legs, white sheaths forming around my bones.

I must have slept, though, for some hours later I woke to find that the snow had stopped and the cloud cover had thinned away, and a late-winter moon was visible above the mountains: just a little off full, with a hangnail missing on the right side, and stars swarming round it. I got up, and did a little dance on the tarn, partly to get warm, and partly because if I looked backwards over my shoulder while I danced, I could see my moon-shadow jigging with me on the snow.

I appreciated the effort that the moonlight had made to reach me. It had left the sun at around 186,000 miles per second, and had then proceeded through space for eight minutes, or ninety-three million miles, and had then upped off the moon's surface and proceeded through space for another 1.3 seconds, or 240,000 miles, before pushing through troposphere, stratosphere and atmosphere, and descending on me: trillions of lunar photons pelting on to my face and the snow about me, giving me an eyeful of silver, and helping my moon-shadow to dance.

I had woken into a metal world. The smooth unflawed slopes of snow on the mountains across the valley were iron. The deeper moon-shadows had a tinge of steel blue to them. Otherwise, there was no true colour. Everything was greys, black, sharp silver-white. Inclined sheets of ice gleamed like tin. The hailstones lay about like shot, millions of them, grouped up against each rock and clustered in snow hollows. The air smelt of minerals and frost. Where I had been lying on the tarn, the ice had melted, so that there was a shallow indent, shaped like a sarcophagus, shadowed out by the moonlight.

To the south, the mountain ridge curved gently round for two miles. It was as narrow as a pavement at times, at others as wide as a road, with three craggy butte summits in its course. To the east and west, the steep-sided valleys, unreachable by the moonlight, were in such deep black shadow that the mountains seemed footless in the world.

I began walking the ridge. The windless cold burnt the edges of my face. These were the only sounds I could hear: the swish of my breathing, the crunch my foot made when it broke through a crust of hard snow, and the wood-like groans of ice sinking as I stepped down on it. I passed an ice dune which was as smooth and glassy as the sill of a weir. My shadow fell for yards behind me. Once, stopping on a crag-top, I watched two stars fall in near parallel down the long black slope of the sky.

When I came to a big frozen pool of water, I took a sharp stone and cut a cone-shaped hole in the white ice where it seemed thinnest. Dark water glugged up into the hole, and I knelt, dipped my mouth to the ice and drank. I caught up a handful of snow, and patted and shaped it in my hands as I walked, so that it shrank and hardened into a small white stone of ice.

Where the ground steepened, I moved from rock to rock to gain purchase. On the thinner sections I walked out to the east, so I could look along the cornice line, which was fine and delicate, and proceeded in a supple curve along the ridge edge and over the moon trench, as if it had been engineered.

Several small clouds drifted through the sky. When one of them passed before the moon, the world's filter changed. First my hands were silver and the ground was black. Then my hands were black and the ground silver. So we switched, as I walked, from negative to positive to negative, as the clouds passed before the moon.

---

The human eye possesses two types of photo-receptive cells: rods and cones. The cone cells cluster in the fovea, the central area of the retina. Further out from the fovea, the density of cone cells diminishes, and rod cells come to predominate. Cone cells are responsible for our acute vision, and for colour perception. But they work well only under bright light conditions. When light levels drop, the eye switches to rod cells.

In 1979, three scientists, Lamb, Baylor and Yau, proved that a rod cell could be tripped into action by the impact of a single photon. They used a suction electrode to record the membrane current of pieces of toad retina with high rod-cell density. They then fired single photons at the retinal pieces. The membrane current showed pronounced fluctuations. It is agreed that this is among the most beautiful experiments in the field of optics.

It takes rod cells up to two hours to adapt most fully to the dark. Once the body detects reduced light levels, it begins generating a photosensitive chemical called rhodopsin, which builds up in the rod cells in a process known as dark adaptation.

So it is that at night, we in fact become more optically sensitive. Night sight, though it lacks the sharpness of day sight, is a heightened form of vision. I have found that on very clear nights, even at sea-level, it is possible to sit and read a book.

Rod cells work with efficiency in low light levels. However, they do not perceive colour – only white, black and the greyscale between. Greyscale is their approximation of colour: 'ghosting in' is what optic scientists call the effect of rod-cell perception. It is for this reason that the world seems drained of colour by moonlight, expressing itself instead in subtle but melancholy shades.

The brightest of all nightscapes is to be found when a full moon shines on winter mountains. Such a landscape offers the maximum reflection, being white, planar, tilted and polished. The only difficulty for the night-walker comes when you move into the moon-shadow of a big outcrop, or through a valley, where moon-shadow falls from all sides and the valley floor receives almost no light at all. The steep-sidedness of the valley is exaggerated: you have the sensation of being at the bottom of a deep gorge, and you long to reach the silver tideline of the moonlight again.

To be out by night in a forest, by a river, on a moor, in a field, or even in a city garden, is to know it differently. Colour seems absent, and you are obliged to judge distance and appearance by shade and tone: night sight requires an attentiveness and a care of address undemanded by sunlight.

The astonishment of the night-walker also has to do with the unconverted and limitless nature of the night sky, which in clear weather is given a depth by the stars that far exceeds the depth given to the diurnal sky by clouds. On a cloudless night, looking upwards, you experience a sudden flipped vertigo, the sensation that your feet might latch off from the earth and you might plummet upwards into space. Star-gazing gives us access to orders of events, and scales of time and space, which are beyond our capacity to imagine: it is unsurprising that dreams of humility and reverence have been directed towards the moon and the stars for as long as human culture has recorded itself.

Our disenchantment of the night through artificial lighting may appear, if it is noticed at all, as a regrettable but eventually trivial side-effect of contemporary life. That winter hour, though, up on the summit ridge with the stars falling plainly far above, it seemed to me that our estrangement from the dark was a great and serious loss. We are, as a species, finding it increasingly hard to imagine that we are part of something which is larger than our own capacity. We have come to accept a heresy of aloofness, a humanist belief in human difference, and we suppress wherever possible the checks and balances on us – the reminders that the world is greater than us or that we are contained within it. On almost every front, we have begun a turning away from a felt relationship with the natural world.

The blinding of the stars is only one aspect of this retreat from the real. In so many ways, there has been a prising away of life from place, an abstraction of experience into different kinds of touchlessness. We experience, as no historical period has before, disembodiment and dematerialisation. The almost infinite connectivity of the technological world, for all the benefits that it has brought, has exacted a toll in the coin of contact. We have in many ways forgotten what the world feels like. And so new maladies of the soul have emerged, unhappinesses which are complicated products of the distance we have set between ourselves and the world. We have come increasingly to forget that our minds are shaped by the bodily experience of being in the world – its spaces, textures, sounds, smells and habits – as well as by genetic traits we inherit and ideologies we absorb. A constant and formidably defining exchange occurs between the physical forms of the world around us, and the cast of our inner world of imagination. The feel of a hot dry wind on the face, the smell of distant rain carried as a scent stream in the air, the touch of a bird's sharp foot on one's outstretched palm: such encounters shape our beings and our imaginations in ways which are beyond analysis, but also beyond doubt. There is something uncomplicatedly true in the sensation of laying hands upon sun-warmed rock, or watching a dense mutating flock of birds, or seeing snow fall irrefutably upon one's upturned palm.

The mountaineer Gaston Rebuffat identified a retreat from the real as underway fifty years ago, in his memoir *Starlight and Storm*. And Rebuffat knew the real. He had spent his life in mountains by night and by day. He had bivouacked on north faces, in rock niches, in snow holes, and walked and climbed in all weathers and all hours. Starlight and storm, for Rebuffat, were indispensable energies, for they returned to those who moved through them a sense of the world's own forces and processes. 'In this modern age, very little remains that is real,' he wrote in 1956.

> Night has been banished, so have the cold, the wind, and the stars. They have all been neutralized: the rhythm of life itself is obscured. Everything goes so fast, and makes so much noise, and men hurry by without heeding the grass by the roadside, its colour, its smell ... But what a strange encounter then is that between man and the high places of his planet! Up there he is surrounded by silence. If there is a slope of snow steep as a glass window, he climbs it, leaving behind him a strange trail.

---

After an hour's slow walking, I reached the flat-topped final summit of the ridge. Leading off it to the south-east was a steep little ice couloir, only twenty or thirty feet long, curved up at either edge, and sheeny with clear ice. It led down to a saddle and a small lower top. I sat down and heeled my way to the rim of the couloir, then luged down it, using my feet as breaks, striking ice chips with them, and feeling the cold black air crack against my face as I slid, so that it seemed as though I were passing through shattering plates of ice, until I slowed to a halt. Then I cleared some space among the rocks of the outcrop, pitched by bivouac, and tried to sleep.

Before sunrise I got up, stretched, stamped my feet and blew into my cupped hands. Then I walked over to the hard drifts of snow on the eastern side of the outcrop, and cut a snow seat, in which I sat and watched as dawn, polar and silent, broke over the white mountains.

**When a woman writes in to ask for help with dealing with her terror of the dark, she encounters an unlikely fellow sufferer – Mariella herself.**

---

# Dear Mariella

THE DILEMMA: *I am 27, and it feels childish to admit, but I am still afraid of the dark. I am a very confident and assertive woman who has no problem walking home alone at night, but when I am in my room at night, I feel reduced to the state of a child. My mind races with images and thoughts that stop me from falling asleep. Shadows scare me, as do sounds. I don't drink too much coffee, I exercise regularly and never watch horror films. There doesn't seem to be a reason for this phobia. With my partner I sleep fine. But he is working away from home, and for the past few months I haven't been able to sleep. This was a problem throughout my teenage years. I thought I'd shrugged it off in my early 20s, but it seems to have come back worse than ever.*

How interesting – me, too! I know you all presume me to be perfect, but really, I have hidden depths. Ever since I can remember, the moment darkness sets in, my imagination, pretty dull during the day, goes into fecund overdrive. It's the reason I've never lived in a house in the city and have to get my mum to sleep over if I'm alone at our remote cottage in Scotland. The nonsensical presumption that my elderly parent is going

MARIELLA FROSTRUP

to be a deterrent to the sort of serial murderers I imagine roaming the moors is proof of the irrationality of such a phobia. Think John Ryder crossed with Ted Bundy but nastier – that's the sort of guy I know is out there creeping through the darkness, miles from civilisation and looking for *me*! Talk about delusional.

Now, despite inhabiting a sixth-floor eyrie in an apartment block, I have an alarm system that can compete with the Bank of England's. Even when my husband is home, chain, locks and alert button all have to be in place before there's a hope of me going to sleep. Despite the Broadmoor-style security I *still* wake up in the middle of the night and imagine intruders and noises. If I say to you my phobia has improved enormously since I was your age you'll understand how bad it was!

I love your list of sensible lifestyle choices pitted against the irrationality of your fear of the dark. We all want to believe that doing the right thing leads to resolution, but the complicated machinations of the human brain far outmanoeuvre our efforts to achieve a semblance of control over our psyche. I've no doubt that this is a serious phobia that deserves expert help, but I've never got round to tackling it. Now I'm starting to wonder if I shouldn't follow my own advice for once because, quite honestly, I'm sick to death of being so scared. I've often wondered about hypnosis, as the reports I've had back from those who have sought a 'talking cure' have been less than inspiring. Acquaintances have spent years in therapy trying to 'remember' their trauma, only to have it ascribed to an evil obstetrician brandishing forceps or some such – and still they're shrieking at shadows.

There is something primordial about fearing what we can't see; that's life in a nutshell! You could just accept that you have a flaw, as I have, which is that in this area I'm no more mature than my six-year-old son. His solution to combat the monsters he fears in the night is to sleep with an array of plastic weaponry: swords, daggers, machetes and so on. They lie arrayed on his pillow in a heart-breaking display of vulnerability, a mark of my hopelessness as a parent in eradicating his fear. I take some comfort from the fact that it's the same penchant for imaginative play, often involving little more than a stick and a scrap of discarded fake fur from his sister's lion costume, that sustains him during the daylight hours.

Can we take heart from the fact that it means we are maybe superior imaginative beings? Perhaps if we lose our fear of the dark we lose other parts of our make up that we would be less pleased to dispense with? I did throw your question out to Twitterland to see if we are unique in our terror; the result was a resounding 'no'. Curiously no men admitted to being scared, but an avalanche of women, including many feisty gals from Caitlin Moran to Sarah Vine, came back with stories of their own night fears. If there are cures out there hopefully this column will attract answers. For now it seems to me there are only two answers: wipe out all men (I'm not alone in *never* having imagined a knife-wielding woman in my bedroom) or try hypnotherapy. I'll be going for the latter first. How about you?

---

Mariella Frostrup: *Dear Mariella* (2012).

# I WAKE AND FEEL THE FELL OF DARK, NOT DAY

Gerard Manley Hopkins

I WAKE and feel the fell of dark, not day.
What hours, O what black hoürs we have spent
This night! what sights you, heart, saw; ways you went!
And more must, in yet longer light's delay.
With witness I speak this. But where I say
Hours I mean years, mean life. And my lament
Is cries countless, cries like dead letters sent
To dearest him that lives alas! away.

I am gall, I am heartburn. God's most deep decree
Bitter would have me taste: my taste was me;
Bones built in me, flesh filled, blood brimmed the curse.
Selfyeast of spirit a dull dough sours. I see
The lost are like this, and their scourge to be
As I am mine, their sweating selves; but worse.

# 3 AM PLAYLIST

## Bryan Biggs

The creative pull of the nocturnal hours on artists extends beyond visual art and literature. In popular music for instance, the night has a thousand eyes, you could be swinging on a star, and the moon is blue, pink or yellow, rising badly and inspiring moon rivers and moondances. For Ray Charles the night-time is the right time, for the KLF 3 a.m. is eternal. From Don MacLean's starry, starry night to Joanna Newsom's explication of the difference between meteor, meteorite and meteoroid in her song *Emily*, songwriters have found inspiration in the night sky. The early hours are particularly fruitful: Leonard Cohen's *Famous Blue Raincoat* letter penned at four in the morning, whilst Pérez Prado even made a whole album of dangerous Cuban rhythms, *Havana, 3 a.m.,*

MC 54 56 58 60 62 64 68 72 76

MC 54 55 65 70 80

**Frank Crumit** *Three O'Clock In The Morning* (1922)
**B. B. King** *3 O'Clock Blues* (1950)
**Santo & Johnny** *Sleepwalk* (1958)
**Bobby Lewis** *Tossin' and Turnin'* (1961)
**Simon & Garfunkel** *Wednesday Morning, 3 A.M.* (1964)
**The Move** *Night of Fear* (1966)
**The Electric Prunes** *I Had Too Much To Dream (Last Night)* (1966)
**The Pretty Things** *Walking Through My Dreams* (1968)
**David McWilliams** *3 O'Clock Flamingo Street* (1969)
**The 5th Dimension** *(Last Night) I Didn't Get to Sleep at All* (1972)

MC

in 1956, though it contains no song of that title. In the Everly Brothers' famous single, it's four o'clock and little Susie is in deep trouble if she doesn't wake up soon; and at sixty-four, will we stay out till a quarter to three, as in the Beatles song? Searching songs on the Internet on the subject of 3 a.m. unearths a staggering number of efforts thus titled, many seemingly written at that hour by lovelorn, lonely or insomniac individuals. Most are instantly forgettable. Others offer dance remixes in the chill of the night, creating that 3 a.m. mood for the wired raver. Spurning these in favour of a more eclectic, historical selection, the nocturnal tunes below aim to capture something of the wonder and paranoia of the restless night.

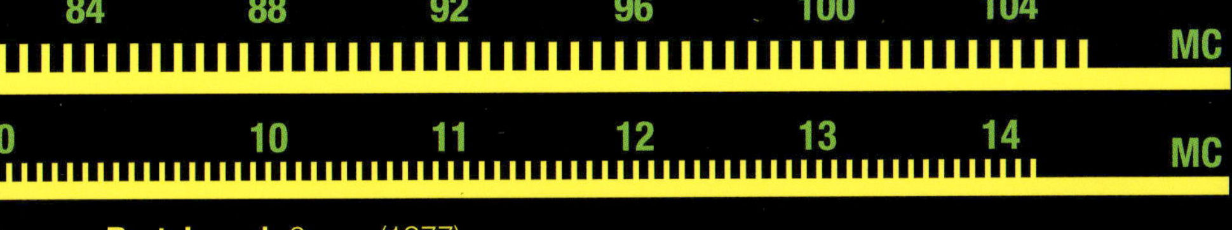


**Bert Jansch** *3 a.m.* (1977)
**John Martyn** *Small Hours* (1977)
**The KLF** *3 A.M. Eternal* (1989)
**11:59** *3 AM* (1990)
**Orbital** *2 Deep* (1990)
**Faithless** *Insomnia* (1995)
**Depeche Mode** *The Dead Of Night* (2001)
**Laura Marling** *Night Terror* (2008)
**Eminem** *3 a.m.* (2009)
**Elbow** *The Night Will Always Win* (2011)

MC

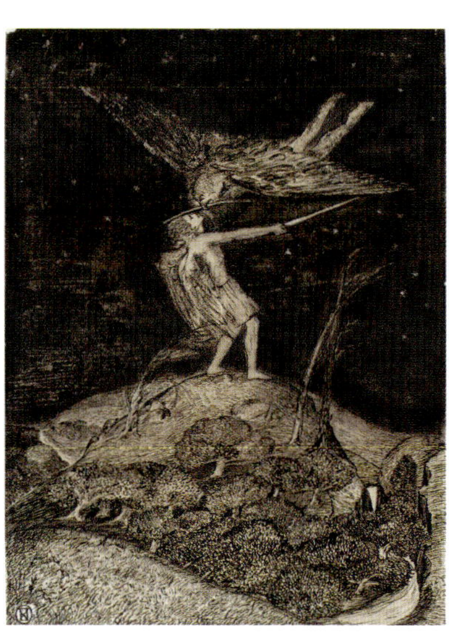

Paul Nash (1889–1946)
*The Combat/Angel and Devil*, 1910
Pencil, ink and wash
Reproduced with kind permission of V&A Images/Victoria and Albert Museum, London. ©Tate, London 2012

# ACKNOWLEDGEMENTS

The editor would like to thank Angela Kingston, the curator of *3am: wonder, paranoia and the restless night*, who suggested much of the content of this publication. Special thanks also go to: the artists for participating in the exhibition and giving permission to reproduce their work here; to the writers who have written new texts, as well as those whose existing texts we have included; to the galleries who have lent artworks to the exhibition and given permission to reproduce images here; to the publishers who have granted permission to use extracts of texts; and to the galleries who have agreed to host the exhibition on its UK tour, following the initial showing in Liverpool.

Angela Kingston would like to thank Bryan Biggs, Denise Courcoux, Caroline Maclennan and Sara-Jayne Parsons, the exhibitions team at the Bluecoat. They have made this an exceptional curatorial commission, characterised by far-reaching discussion and ambitious thinking in these straitened times; and they have taken the creative lead on this publication and a related programme of *3am* events. She would also like to thank Marion Coutts, Charles Darwent, Colin Dilnot, Victoria Hardie, Elizabeth Humby, Hazel Mills, Malcolm Robertson and Hugh Stoddart for their support and ideas.